THE JAZZ PILGRIMAGE OF GERALD WILSON

THE JAZZ PILGRIMAGE OF

GERALD WILSON

STEVEN LOZA

FOREWORD BY ANTHONY WILSON

UNIVERSITY PRESS OF MISSISSIPPI / JACKSON

www.upress.state.ms.us

Designed by Peter D. Halverson

The University Press of Mississippi is a member of the
Association of University Presses.

First printing 2018

∞

Library of Congress Cataloging-in-Publication Data

Names: Loza, Steven Joseph, author.
Title: The jazz pilgrimage of Gerald Wilson / Steven Loza; foreword by
Anthony Wilson.
Description: Jackson: University Press of Mississippi, 2018. | Series:
American made music series | Includes bibliographical references and
index. |
Identifiers: LCCN 2017038269 (print) | LCCN 2017040133 (ebook) | ISBN
9781496816030 (epub single) | ISBN 9781496816047 (epub institutional)
| ISBN 9781496816054 (pdf single) | ISBN 9781496816061 (pdf
institutional) | ISBN 9781496816023 (cloth)
Subjects: LCSH: Wilson, Gerald, 1918-2014. | Composers—United
States—Biography. | Jazz musicians—United States—Biography. | Band
directors—United States—Biography.
Classification: LCC ML410.W7147 (ebook) | LCC ML410.W7147 L69 2018 (print) |
DDC 781.65092 [B]—dc23
LC record available at https://lccn.loc.gov/2017038269

British Library Cataloging-in-Publication Data available

DEDICATED TO
GERALD AND JOSEFINA

CONTENTS

ACKNOWLEDGMENTS

I would like to express my gratitude to the UCLA Academic Senate and the UCLA Herb Alpert School of Music for research grants and stipends to assist me in the research and completion of this book, especially Jeri, Nancy Jo, Anthony, and Eric.

I also acknowledge with great thanks my research assistants, who have been indispensable in making this project come to fruition. They include Dr. Francisco Crespo, Dr. Kathleen Hood, Eric Otis, and Varo Galstyan.

A great amount of thanks and respect is also due to the editors at the University Press of Mississippi, especially director Craig Gill, who has supported this project in a very gracious and personal way, and copyeditor Peter Tonguette. I would also like to express my sincere respect for the anonymous evaluations of the manuscript. I am very grateful to the two readers.

Finally, I am indebted to the Wilson family for all their giving and involvement in the writing of the book, especially Jeri, Anthony, and Eric.

And, of course, to the project's two principal fountains of information, knowledge, and wisdom, my total respect and love go to Gerald and Josefina. I know they rest in peace and love.

FOREWORD

Century of Progress

In the Mississippi Delta, on both sides of the famous north-south Route 61, the land stretches out flatly, and tiny towns with vivid names like Ruleville, Renova, Merigold, Mound Bayou, Hushpuckena, Alligator, and Lula scroll by like credits in an old movie. Recently, I took a trip to the area to visit Shelby, the town where my father Gerald Wilson—the subject of this book—was born. I felt like I was going back in time. The sky was vast and cloudless, and people with whom I had even the most fleeting of conversations were disarmingly direct and kind. I stood at the site of my father's early home and the adjacent schoolhouse where his mother (my grandmother) taught, just across the street from the old rail depot; and I saw the tin shed in which his father (my grandfather) plied his trade as a blacksmith. Throughout this region, the legacy of the old brutal southern strain of racial oppression is something you can feel, and the effect of decades of economic neglect is something you can see. There is a profound and mystical quality to the place. This world nurtured the otherworldly blues wail heard on 1920s and 1930s recordings by musicians like Robert Johnson, Charlie Patton, Son House, and Skip James. The Mississippi Delta's unique combination of panoramic vista and intensely expressive sound, I believe, is the deep taproot of Gerald Wilson's consciousness and art, which nourished him throughout his life and career.

I know I'm not alone in having long hoped for a volume like this about my dad's life and music. I am a jazz musician myself, and I have been fortunate to have the experience of traveling around the world and to hear firsthand from other musicians, arts presenters, students, scholars, and fans, the deep and lasting imprint my father—as a person and an artist—made on their lives. People treasure their memories of his performances, recounting stories of seeing his unique and powerful orchestra at the Lighthouse or Basin Street East or the Vienna Konzerthaus; completists voraciously collect his records from every stage of his career; former students tell me about taking his Development of Jazz class at one university or another; Angelenos recall listening to *Jazz Capsule*, his great radio interview show of the 1970s on LA's KBCA. More than anything else, the people I meet who had a chance to know him always reminisce about my father's true kindness and gentleness.

This book combines oral history, personal biography, cultural scholarship, discography, and musical analysis. We hear stories about my father's boyhood in Mississippi and Memphis, his student days in Detroit, and his first forays as a professional musician. Remembered names of people, bands, and places are summoned forth from my father's memory in vivid detail. The very important sense of musical, cultural, and social evolution over a period of ninety years, which helped shape him as a person, is rendered here too. What it took for him to recalibrate himself with a period of musical *hunkering down* after his first early successes between 1939 and 1945, a huge personal decision which led to a deepening of his music and an expanding of his professional possibilities, is recounted, and as readers we are given the opportunity to track Gerald Wilson's path to maturity and to his mid- and late-career accomplishments.

In 1933 and 1934, a World's Fair known as "A Century of Progress" was held in Chicago to celebrate that city's centennial. It was a huge event meant to highlight the positive impact that science, technology, and industry were having on peoples' lives. Held during the Great Depression, it reflected a spirit of optimism at a time when the country was digging itself out of massive hardship. After living in the south for fifteen years, Gerald Wilson was given the opportunity to travel to Chicago with close family friends, the Trouts. Though the city was still segregated, the teen-aged aspiring musician sensed possibility there that he certainly never could have imagined in Shelby. This defining moment set him on a path to find freedom in new ideas, possibilities, and locales, and took him on the journey recounted in this book. In a musical career encompassing seventy-five years and a life spanning ninety-six years, my father always sought something more, something further, something deeper. For Gerald Wilson, it was a century of progress indeed.

Anthony Wilson
Los Angeles, November 2016

PROLOGUE

Must we, really, assume that philosophers have been able to penetrate into the purpose and power of God, while the Prophets could not?
— SAINT AUGUSTINE

The "jazz pilgrimage" of Gerald Wilson not only supplies this book with its title; it is the verbal metaphor that Gerald Wilson used for many years to describe his life, his goals, and his mission in the world of jazz.

What I remember hearing in Gerald's music was what we used to say back then, that "black and beautiful" feel, especially in his charts such as John Coltrane's "Equinox" or his own piece named for his wife and the introductory theme to his radio show, "Josefina." All of this filled me with a feeling of great hope, great emotion, and great pride. I will not nor can I ever forget that feeling, which lives with me to this day.

Years later, when I was writing my book *Barrio Rhythm: Mexican American Music in Los Angeles*, I realized in part why this man was so essential in my life. He in many ways epitomized my musical experience, my goals, and most of all, my culture. "Viva Tirado," recorded by the group El Chicano in 1970, was one of the essential recordings, almost a hymn, during and after the Chicano movement, and it was composed by Gerald Wilson. I continued to feel this *closeness* to Gerald. It seemed that we shared this affinity, these intersections of the African American, the Latin, and the need for experimentation, for extension, for loving the idea of crossing over, of sharing, of creating.

For me to be involved in the writing of this book is an honor and gives me a feeling of great fulfillment, both as a musician and as a junior colleague and student of Gerald. But there is even more poetry to all of this. In the mid-1970s, when I was a student of composition and jazz studies at Cal Poly Pomona, I used to religiously listen to Gerald Wilson's *Jazz Capsule* radio program on KBCA. I still vividly remember listening to Gerald interview jazz artists such as Freddie Hubbard, Chick Corea, Bobby Rodriguez, Garrett Sarracho, among many others. I was a young jazz freak wanting to eat up all the music, and even more so, the culture that Gerald represented and gave to us over the airwaves. He was a teacher in everything he did.

I used to go see the Gerald Wilson Orchestra as often as I could. I saw him and his band perform at McArthur Park and at the Pilgrimage Theatre—yes, the "Pilgrimage," now called the Ford Amphitheatre. It was after a Pilgrimage concert that I went and found Gerald, coming out the walkway from the theater. I had specifically brought with me a reel-to-reel tape of my music recorded by the Cal Poly Jazz Band in addition to that of my senior recital (I had just completed my bachelor's degree in music at Cal Poly Pomona). My musical ideals and style had been highly impacted by the music and persona of Gerald Wilson, and I wanted him to hear my music.

It would be close to twenty years later, in the mid-1990s, that I was teaching at UCLA as a young professor, and magically, Gerald had become my colleague. He had begun teaching the History of Jazz class to our students (classes that reached five hundred students at a time). One day I asked Gerald if he still had the reel-to-reel tape of the music I had given him way back when, as I had lost my original copies and wanted to work them into a CD recording I was producing of my earlier compositions. Gerald came back to me shortly thereafter, and to my delight and relief, he told me that he had found the tape. He also told me that he took the time to listen to it; in fact, he "listened to every note." Talk about lighting a fire under my pants!

The tape did evolve into my new CD. But just as important, I was reunited with my master mentor in an extremely unique and blessed way. Since that time, Gerald and I began to work together and to hold an ongoing discourse, talking about jazz culture, Latino culture, politics, American society, race, our families, the world, and so much more. Gerald had become my colleague, but he was still my mentor, and I cherished the role and beamed with pride just to be able to be so close to him. We worked on projects together at UCLA, in Mexico, in New Mexico, and ultimately, on this very book.

I will forever remember something Gerald Wilson always said: "Always tell the truth."

In actuality, Gerald and I have written this book. Gerald's words tell us his story. My job has been to structure our interviews and the other sources into a manuscript in which different points are made and different stories told. You will notice that at various points in the manuscript I may speak as "we," depending on the context. Gerald, of course, speaks as he did in the interviews, in the first person, and I will speak in the first or third person from my own point of view. It is somewhat of a macramé, weaving approach of facts, opinions, and ideas. It can be considered a bit of an experiment, but I feel it is a unique and valid writing style.

THE JAZZ PILGRIMAGE OF GERALD WILSON

CHAPTER 1

TOWARD AN ASSESSMENT OF GERALD WILSON

Jazz criticism, certainly as it has existed in the United States, has served in a great many instances merely to obfuscate what has actually been happening with the music itself.
—LEROI JONES (AMIRI BARAKA)

In this book, Gerald Wilson and I have set out to present a perspective on his life, an artistic life that he has for many years referred to as his "jazz pilgrimage." Gerald Wilson's journey has been one that has defied many categories, especially those developed by critics attempting to divide the concept of jazz and its great innovators into specified notches, thereby often ascribing limits on the effect of an artist. In the case of Gerald Wilson, such categorization has been evasive, as he cannot be specified into a notch. He is simply too transcendent for such nonsense.

The life and work of Gerald Wilson has been highlighted by numerous and diverse creative stages, events, compositions, recordings, performances, honors, awards, and professional roles. He has been musician, composer, arranger, orchestrator, conductor, trumpeter, producer, radio program host, educator, writer, husband, and father. All of this, however, has been cradled and nurtured through the world and legacy of what we call jazz, and it is in this spirit that we have attempted to present here a historical testament and meditation on Wilson's work and its impact on humanity.

GERALD WILSON IN THE JAZZ LITERATURE

There has been debate as to whether Gerald Wilson, among other jazz artists based on the West Coast, has been given sufficient attention in the press, especially that of what might be referred to as the jazz literature. In his book *West Coast Jazz: Modern Jazz in California*, Ted Gioia notes that "the story of West Coast big bands from the 1950s, especially those featuring black leaders, was largely one of neglect . . . Gerald Wilson was one of the more talented and stylized West Coast bandleaders of the postwar years" (Gioia 1992: 141). Alyn Shipton, in his *A New History of Jazz*, makes a similar observation, noting that "Gerald Wilson is one of the most accomplished and overlooked figures in jazz history" (Shipton 2001: 514). Although Wilson is cited and profiled in major encyclopedic works and a number of jazz magazines, in addition to some excellent and extensive, more recent CD liner notes by Doug Ramsey and Kirk Silsbee, numerous books focusing on contemporary jazz artists have completely ignored him and his work.

One theory that has been suggested as to why this situation exists is based on the idea that West Coast jazz was not mainstreamed in the mostly East Coast-quartered jazz literature; thus, Wilson and others in California did not receive a balanced attention and analysis from the press. This theory, however, does not "jibe" with the historical record of artists such as Chet Baker, Gerry Mulligan, Stan Kenton, and many other West Coast jazz artists that did and continue to receive extensive press and critical coverage. The issue of race, as noted above by Gioia, may be an issue that pervades this paradox.

SCOPE OF THE BOOK

I hope that this book can represent Wilson's ideas as related to music and life, with all of their philosophical, historical, and cultural relationships. Whether or not this book should be considered an academic work is a subjective issue. It "is" and "is not" part of the academic world.

We have based the book on a diversity of sources and concepts. The primary source has been the testimony of Wilson himself, which I have compiled and organized through a series of interviews[1] and dialogues that we have conducted. In addition to this, I have collected and combed through a variety of documented sources, including recordings by Wilson's orchestra or other ensembles and published interviews and essays directly focusing on Wilson or referring to him in the context of more general sources, e.g., recordings in which he participated or essays or books on other topics that have referred to his artistic oeuvre. One unique source that I have also tapped is an oral interview conducted with Wilson and released on a spoken word double album produced by the MAMA Foundation (*Suite Memories: Reflections on a Jazz Journey,* 1996).

I have organized the book into sections that in some cases are based on chronological events and stages in the development and career of Gerald Wilson, while in other cases, specific sociocultural themes or musical analysis. Wilson's early life and education are addressed in chapter 2, while chapter 3 focuses on his experience with the Jimmie Lunceford orchestra through the formation of Wilson's own and first orchestra. In chapter 4, Wilson describes the reasons he abandoned his early and highly successful musical career to study more music, and chapter 5 proceeds to highlight the maestro's San Francisco and Los Angeles orchestras, specifically putting into context his many recordings on the Pacific Jazz Records label. Chapter 6 highlights Wilson's consistent, progressive development during the second part of his career that encompassed various phases and explorations, including active work in media and education. Chapter 7 takes an in-depth look at a very significant aspect of his life and music, that of Latino culture. In chapter 8, I present a diverse selection of musical profiles reflecting Wilson's evolution in musical style, composition, and arranging. I conclude the book with chapter 9, where I reflect on Wilson's impact on music and the world, and the way in which he accomplished this. Here I refer to and borrow ideas of scholars and thinkers who have philosophized on concepts and historical issues that I feel are highly relevant to the work of Gerald Wilson.

Wilson's life has progressed through and in many places, representing different time periods, beginning with his birthplace of Shelby, Mississippi, to Memphis, Detroit, New York City, Chicago, the Great Lakes Naval

---

1. A series of interviews was conducted by the author with Gerald Wilson in 2001. The interviews were videotaped by David Martinelli, technician in the UCLA Department of Ethnomusicology.

Station, San Francisco, and his home, Los Angeles. His many awards and recognitions will be cited in this historical record; but our purpose is to go further than the external recognition and what is too frequently merely description and analysis. It is our hope that we can let you into the heart and soul of Gerald Wilson, and to do some serious experimentation and innovation with this book—perhaps in the way that the maestro has made music throughout his life.

Wilson passed away during the last stages of completing this book. It is dedicated to him and his family, and to the life that he continues to give us.

CHAPTER 2

THE PILGRIMAGE OF YOUTH

Children are not blank slates for a teacher to write on. Nor are they empty vessels into which we pour knowledge. They are already called to a destiny that is about something great and beautiful.

—LUIS RODRIGUEZ

Before we started the first interview for this book, I commented to Wilson on something he had mentioned to me some days earlier. He had told me that he does not consider himself a genius. I took this moment, before we started our interview, to tell him that I did not agree with his statement, and I expressed my view as follows:

Loza: I think genius comes in different forms. Gerald Wilson, in addition to being a musician of the highest level in our musical world, is also a man that has other kinds of values and opinions and family knowledge and family history that transcends just the art . . . and like we were just talking about, the eyes being related to all parts of the body, everything is related to everything else in this life that we live . . . you can't just yank out the music as a subject.

Wilson agreed to speak about his life.

Wilson: I was born in a little town in Mississippi, and the name of that town is Shelby. It is one hundred miles from Memphis, Tennessee. It's twenty-seven miles from Clarksdale, Mississippi. And I would say that it is also seven miles from a town called Mound Bayou, Mississippi, and

7

the reason I mention Mound Bayou is because it's important in my life. I went there many times. Mound Bayou, by the way, happened to at that time have been an all-black town. The mayor. The doctors . . . everybody there. It was a black city. They had their own school. So I spent many days there. I was born to my mother and father. My father's name was Shelby, the same name as the town. He was named Shelby J. Wilson. His father (who I don't know where he was born but I imagine it might have been in Shelby), his name was also Shelby Wilson. And my brother's name is also Shelby Wilson. My mother was born in Selma, Alabama. She graduated from a school in Jackson, Mississippi. Now it's called Jackson State College but it was called just Jackson College in those days. And it seems to me that from the time she was born, I mean from the time she was out of school, she began her career and life being a teacher. She taught in Shelby for many years. She also taught in a few other places. She taught in a place called Laurel, Mississippi, for a year. And she taught in a place called Duncan, Mississippi, which is not too far from Shelby . . . about eight miles. And she also taught in a place called Hushpuckena, Mississippi, which is just four miles north of Shelby. Well, her mother, whose name was Nancy Wilson, owned a store in Hushpuckena. So that was my mother's home when she was with her. So that's how Hushpuckena comes in on the scene . . . a place that I spent many days during my lifetime as a young boy. So that was one of the important places. I have a brother whose name, as I said, is Shelby. And I had a sister whose name was Mildred Wilson. My brother . . . I remember as a kid, my brother, he started into grammar school. They only had a grammar school in Shelby when I was there. So this meant that once you finished the grammar school you had to go someplace else to continue your education. As I said, my brother and sister both attended school until they graduated from grammar school and then they attended other schools. My brother attended high school in Clarksdale, which I've explained is twenty-seven miles north of Shelby. And my sister, after she graduated from grammar school, she also continued her education in Clarksdale for a couple of years or so. Clarksdale became very important in my family's life because my sister is a classical pianist. By the way, I might add to this, my mother could play the piano. She could read music. She played for the church. She played for the school when we needed her (things that they have at the average school). And she started all of her children off on the piano, me included.

I was very small, maybe about four or five years old. She taught us how to read music and how to begin. As an instrument, we played the piano a bit. My brother did very well with that and my sister did exceptionally well. She became a classical pianist. So this really brought Clarksdale in on the picture because of her music teacher and her husband, Mr. Mosley. Mrs. Mosley taught music at the school in Clarksdale called Agricultural High School. Mr. Mosley was the principal of this school. Incidentally, his son finally moved to Los Angeles and became a teacher in the school system here, in Los Angeles. Mr. Mosley, the principal of the Agricultural High School, later became the president of a school in Atlanta, Georgia, called Morehouse College. I'm sure you've heard of Morehouse. It's one of the oldest Negro colleges in the world and a highly recognized school. So they came in to play very important parts in the life of the Wilson family. I remember as a child, I must have been maybe three or four years old, we would have to travel to Clarksdale to go and take my sister, a couple of years or so that we could go get her lessons on the piano. In the meantime, as I said, my brother attended some high school in Clarksdale also and then moved on to Tuskegee, Alabama, to go to Tuskegee Institute there. This is the institute that was founded by, of course, Booker T. Washington. I don't know if you've heard of him but he was a man that was born a slave and in time when he was free he founded this Negro institute . . . this school, which has become very prominent in the world . . . surely for black people. But not only for black people. For a lot of people. And it's a school that the great scientist George Washington Carver was teaching there. It's the first school that was chosen to teach the first black pilots in America. And so this is a very prominent school.

I bring all this up because it also plays a part in my life. My brother attended school and graduated from that school. He graduated from Tuskegee in 1929 and knew Teddy Wilson [whose father was the head of the English Department there, and whose mother was the librarian there]. Teddy Wilson of course becoming one of the greatest jazz pianists of all time [and who studied music at Talladega College, also in Alabama]. He and my brother were friends. I can remember looking in my brother's annual the year that he graduated [and remembering that] the family was friends with my brother. Teddy had a brother named Gus Wilson, a fine trombone player, which you'd find, I'm sure, in some music books around. In fact, my brother said that Duke Ellington one time wanted to get Gus

Wilson. His name was very important in the world of fine trombonists. But anyway, as I said, this plays a big part because my brother was an avid jazz fan and enthusiast. As I said, he could play some piano and he had a knack about getting music done. In fact, he's the one that actually inspired me to want to be a musician. He would tell me all about the great musicians all around the world. Jazz musicians. He would tell me about Duke Ellington, tell me all about Cab Calloway . . . all about the bands. The Mills Blue Ribbon band. Chick Webb. All the great bands. Earl Hines. Erskine Tate. Carol Dickson. These were the bands that were very good in those days. In fact, in those days everything was black or white so they would be the black bands or white bands. So these were some of the black bands that were very popular. And we would stay up at night listening to the bands as they broadcast from New York and Chicago and whatever cities they would be in at that time. And I became very obsessed with jazz, and was wanting to be a jazz musician. He had all of the records. Not only black records but he had records of all the people that played jazz, [and bandleaders like] Freddy Waring, around the house. Bix Beiderbecke and Frankie Trumbauer, who had their bands out. Vincent Lopez . . . Carlos Molina, Herbie Cade, and all those bands. We listened to all of them. We'd buy records by Louis Armstrong, of course. And, of course, he had Duke and Earl and all those people. And we were both so inspired with jazz. I just loved for him to tell me the stories and we would listen to the radio broadcast and play the records. Eventually, of course . . . this was during the time I had already started school myself.

By the age of five, I was already listening to these people. I was born in 1918, right at the end of World War I. And I saw many of the soldiers that came back that lived in Shelby. They'd come back from the war. And I saw things happening around . . . you know, at the time I was very inquisitive about it. I had begun to wonder why we were segregated. Why that we couldn't drink out of this fountain or that fountain. Why if we went to the movies that we had to sit in a separate place. I began to think about it because these things . . . you hear things from not only from your parents but from your associates. My friends, they were talking about things like that, and I became very inquisitive about it, I'd say at the year that I finished the fourth grade . . . that would be about 1927. To keep up with [my memories of] my sister's music lessons, the Mosleys took on a job in a place called Laurel, Mississippi. Professor Mosley as again being the principal, and Mrs. Mosley, the music teacher of the school. It was called Queensburg Jr. High School or something like that. The grades started at sixth grade. I had just finished the fourth grade so my mother took me at that time in 1927, when I was about eight years old. I think my father left when I was about eight. My mother had to go to Laurel. She took a job there to teach there with the Mosleys so that my sister could still be with her teacher, her piano teacher, Mrs. Mosley. This was a great experience because this was in Laurel, Mississippi, another place that I hadn't been. And so my mother just moved me from the fourth grade to the sixth grade because that's where it started at this school. And it didn't bother me too much. Having been with my mother all the time in school, I knew many things the average kid wouldn't know because I'd been with my mother in school. Even as a child before I started going to grammar school. So it was no big deal. Actually, I was able to pass the grade and everything, but I skipped the fifth grade completely. So we spent a wonderful year there in Laurel, Mississippi. And I met some friends there . . . people that had been into music, two or three of my friends in school. One of them was a piano player. His name was . . . I can remember his name because I was talking to a few people even back in the seventies . . . Edward Figuero. And I told him that I had spent a year in Laurel. I said, "But my best friend . . . he played the piano and he only had one finger on his left hand and the rest were just a little nub." They said, "That's Nubby Jackson." They knew who he was. And there were other musicians around the town also that we'd go and watch and follow playing the instruments. I had not yet started to play any other instrument. I was still taking little lessons from my mother . . . piano playing . . . little songs and things like that. So anyway, it was a good time in Laurel Mississippi. My sister was able to keep up her lessons there with the Mosleys.

We returned to Shelby the next year, so this would be 1928. Then that was the year, of course, when the stock market crashed. This is something that I remember, things like . . . I was talking to, maybe it was [a friend named] Martinez, the other day. He remembered people jumping out of the windows when they lost their money in New York, all the big places. So it was a big tragedy and it wasn't too long after that, that things became very tight. Money was tight and banks crashed. Of course, the bank closed and people lost their money. My family along with everybody else lost their money that they had saved. And the same thing happened with my grandmother, who as I said had a store in Hushpuckena. Anyway, trying to put it all together here . . . it was a time when I began to . . . I would seek a few little things around Shelby, my home, where I could help earn money. I'd take a job maybe working at the grocery store delivering groceries. One year my mother took a job at the post office delivering special deliveries. My mother was well respected in the city of Shelby and everybody knew who the Wilson kids were. It was at this time that my mother and my father separated. So it was very hard on my mother, trying to keep my brother in school. As I told you, my brother graduated in 1929. My sister also had graduated from high school and had started going to a college in Jackson, Mississippi, called Tougaloo. It was an all-girls black school. So at this time she had gone to college. So I was doing things to try and help around . . . to help my mother, which she needed very bad. Of course, we received help from her mother who owned the store. So I spent much time with her mother in the store . . . in between we were able to survive. However, during that period my life began to change quite a bit because my mother had a job delivering the special deliveries at the post office, but I was the one who was actually doing the delivering. She would just get the stuff and I would go and deliver it to the people in the town. And as I said, everybody in the town knew me and knew the Wilson family. I played there as a kid with my friends all of the time, but as I said, we were always well protected there.

THE TROUTS AND MEMPHIS

I was kind of afraid during that period because I was getting older and I was afraid of the way things were . . . the hostility towards blacks or the bad things that were happening to blacks around the area, in Alabama, Georgia, and all over in fact, but especially in the southern states. During this period, I used to deliver special deliveries to the Memphis Warehouse Company, a cotton warehouse company. Shelby was the hub of cotton. In fact, at that time they grew more cotton in the area where Shelby was than in any place in the world. It was called the "heart of the delta." It was still a nice time because I enjoyed playing with my friends in the cotton fields.

But to get back to the [warehouse company] . . . I would deliver the special deliveries there every day because they would come from Memphis,

Tennessee. The head company was in Memphis. And these letters would come every day. I would have to deliver this set of special deliveries to the warehouse. This warehouse was run by a husband and wife. Mr. and Mrs. W. E. Trout. They were from Memphis, Tennessee. And one day when I was delivering the special deliveries there, Mrs. Trout said to me, "Gerald, what do you do when you're out of school in the afternoon?" I said, "Well, you know, fool around, play like everybody else, you know," and do all the little things I could do . . . odd jobs around. As I said, I worked sometimes in the store and delivered groceries, and she said, "Well, look, would you ask your mother if you could stay with my son? When he gets out of school we'll bring him over to the house and you will stay with him until we are off in the evening, and we will pay you." So I told my mother about it and my mother agreed. She knew them. She knew the Trouts because she had been delivering some of the stuff there. And so she said it was all right if I wanted to do it. So I didn't see anything wrong with it. The kid, he was a very young kid . . . actually I was more like a baby-sitter, but he was in school already. So I could teach him his lessons, I would teach him things . . . how to take care of himself. And we became very good friends, the kid and I. And also the Trouts became very friendly to me. They would really extend things that I could do because of what I did for the kid. And I actually became very close to the Trouts. They would take me places with them . . . take me to Memphis, Tennessee. They finally took me to Chicago. The Trouts took me to Chicago in '34. But there was a time when it helped out so very much. As I said, they paid me and also they gave me so many things that was not included in the pay. They just gave me many things, including clothes and other things like that. Things had really gotten tough in those days, as I said. My mother and father had separated and I could notice what had happened. During the days when I was a little kid at Christmastime, I would have a lot of gifts and everything . . . little toys to play with. But then all of a sudden we could hardly get anything because people had hardly had any money at all. It was a really tough time. So I wanted to acknowledge the Trouts' interest in me because they encouraged me . . . I had already, as I said, been determined to be a musician. So they inspired me to go on and put a great effort to it. So they even let me . . . the son and I would stay up at nights to listen to the bands. He was interested in bands by that time; he was interested in whatever I liked. And we'd listen to the bands . . . listen to the music. He wanted to be a musician himself at that time. He was thinking about how when he got old enough he would get the clarinet. It went on for a while. It went on from that time, I'd say from 1928 . . . until 1931.

And as I said, they had taken me to Memphis. They knew I wanted to go to Memphis, Tennessee. Of course, I wanted to go to high school after I graduated from grammar school. . . . They had already taken me about the schools there in Memphis. And they would take me out and I could go and hang out . . . and it turns out later, I joined school in Memphis, Tennessee. So, this was a good time, as I said. My mother arranged for me to go to Memphis to go to high school. To do this it was necessary for my mother to call on two friends that had lived in Shelby for many years, and this was a couple. The name of the couple was the Hollises. Gene Hollis and his wife, Viola. They had moved to Memphis and they agreed to take me. I could stay with them. Of course, my mother would have to pay a fee . . . something. But this would be with people that I knew and people that liked me and it was a good time. I was very happy. Memphis was such a large city to me at that time. It was so much more than Shelby . . . so much more than Clarksdale. This was a big city, you know? They had two schools there. I had to go to a school called Manassas High School. First, I wanted to go to Booker T. Washington High School, named after of course the guy that founded Tuskegee . . . because it was a pretty school and they had a band. At Manassas they didn't have a band. It was a school, but it was a good school. And so a group of guys, a group of musicians around that went to school . . . we just kept raising such a fuss that there was no band, that they finally got us a teacher and started to organize the band at the school. And so we did have a band after all. The first year was very strange. I went to school half of the year and all of a sudden I developed malaria fever. So I had to leave and go back to Shelby.

So then in 1932 I went back after I had recovered from my malaria fever. I went back in 1932 and this time, of course, I didn't have any trouble. It was good. We had the band going. Professor Love was the name [of the person] that taught us. He was the man that was the bandleader of the Postmen's band in Memphis and he was teaching us good. He was a trumpet player too, by the way. And so it was good times there at that time. We had a great time there that year and I loved Manassas High School because Manassas High School was the school that

Jimmie Lunceford taught at. He had been a teacher there. He was also the football coach at Manassas High School. And, of course, Jimmie Lunceford started his band in Memphis, Tennessee. They were first called the Chickasaw Syncopators. And so all of this was great. This kept my interest in music, in jazz . . . kept it very high . . . very high-pitched. So '32 went very good. '33, the next year, was very good. Things were developing. Things were getting better too, by the way. And I had many friends in Memphis, young friends, and finished that year there. And I got a chance to go down on Beale Street where I could go to the Beale Street Palace Theatre and see the live acts, the live bands that would come through . . . the black bands, and the artists that would come . . . the dancers and the singers. So it was a fine time and I learned quite a bit there.

I started playing trumpet actually in Memphis. I actually started before I got to Memphis, in Shelby. I got my horn and I didn't have a teacher at that time. There was a trumpet player that taught at the schools. He gave me some pointers that would help me a little bit.

But in Memphis, as I told you, we had a band there. So I was learning fast. We had a little jazz band. I could hear the different bands that would come and play at the school. Like Doug Jenkins in Memphis was one of the great bands. It's the band that Al Hill sang with. And then there was a band called Mandarin Inn Band. Memphis had quite a few bands. I'd get a chance to go and listen to them. But by the time of 1936, I took trumpet from Mr. Burn. He was the trumpet teacher. I had already learned the system. I could already make G's and A's above high C. So I went up real fast. . . .

In 1934 . . . each year when I'd go back to Shelby, I would go back with the Trouts just as if I had been away and come back. So my association with them was even more cemented with companionship. And as I said, they were treating me so fine . . . wanted me to do well . . . wanted me to study, and made sure that I kept up with my music. So that year . . . it would be the last year of the World's Fair in Chicago. The Chicago World's Fair was 1933 and '34. So Mr. Trout (Walter was his name) . . . he decided to go to the World's Fair with his son and Gene Hollis. And so they offered to take me, which they did. They took me to Chicago. And Chicago, I had relatives there, by the way. So when I got there it was like a whole other world. It was this big city. Memphis was a big city to me, you know, but this was really big and they told me exactly what to do. I had cousins and an aunt there. They said, "What you do is you get them to bring you to Sixty-third and South Parkway and then you take the streetcar there and come up to Evans and then you can walk on south from Evans to our home where we live." This is what we did. It was no big deal. At this time, I was already fifteen years old. I was fifteen years old, so I was a big kid. No big deal. I got out and did exactly what they said. We spent a great two weeks there in Chicago. Incidentally, Steve, on the trip you didn't make the whole trip in one day, we stopped in Wilmington, Illinois. So to do that, Trout had to find a place where we could stay. So we knew exactly what to do. You find the black neighborhood, of course, and you find where there's a restaurant and whether there's a rooming house or whatever they had, if there was a hotel. In this particular case there was a rooming house they found and there was a restaurant. And so we spent this evening . . . I spent the night there. And he went there, checked it out, made sure everything was all right with the room where I was to sleep . . . checked whether it was a good restaurant. And he explained to these people that I'd be there for the night and he'd be by to pick me up in the morning. Well, I tell you this part of the story because in the sixties, I went to Illinois State University to do a thing for the week there, you know, in residence there with the band to do a concert with the band in Illinois State. So it was at one of the rehearsals that I said to the leader (I forget his name now), I said, "You know, I've been to this place before when I was a little kid." He said, "You have?" I said, "Well, they took me to a house. This house has a restaurant downstairs by the black neighborhood and they had rooms upstairs." And I said, "It's a very nice place. I remember very well, it was not a rundown place, it was very nice." So he said, "I know exactly where you've been. I'm going to take you over there." And he drove me over to this place and this was the same house that I had stayed. I told you that story so I could tell you how life is and how things were.

That's how it is just a coincidence that I would go back to this place. As a kid I was there. That year, going to Chicago . . . the city was so big and so different even though it was also segregated just like Memphis, just like Shelby, just like Clarksdale . . . no different. But there was much more. So even with that . . . it was a place that I said, "Gee. I've got to come to the North. I've got to get to the North."

Loza: Much more than the South.

Wilson: Yeah, "I'm looking for freedom." I often wondered in my days . . . of course, as a kid I had sold the *Chicago Defender* in my hometown. I had sold the *Pittsburgh Courier*. These are black papers. I sold the *Baltimore Afro-American* and I had sold *Radio Guide*. So I was aware of what was happening in the world. I knew in the North they were fighting for freedom. And this is what I'm looking for. So I went on the trip. After I got back home I told my mother, I said, "You've got to send me to Chicago. I swear that's where I want to be." My being so inquisitive now and I couldn't handle the South. I couldn't handle the South like I used to. And so my mother knew this. And so she said, "Well, I can't send you to Chicago but I can send you to Detroit," because there was a family that lived a couple of doors from us in Shelby and my mother took care of all their business. They had all moved to Detroit. So the couple, with what she did for them, they would take me in Detroit and I could stay with them.

TO DETROIT

Well, that was like a godsend, not being able to go to Chicago, because Detroit was so far ahead. All of the schools were integrated. I went there to go to high school. I started going to Cass Tech in 1934. And I even met musicians who had graduated before that. Like four years before I got there, they had already graduated from that particular school. But all of the high schools were integrated. Northern. Eastern. Northwestern. Miller. Cass Tech. Commerce. All the schools were already integrated. And even other things, more liberal things were happening in Detroit. Do you know that no black band or black ever went to the Trianon or the Aragon Ballroom in Chicago? But in Detroit, one of the finest ballrooms in the world, the Graystone, blacks were already going there. It was their special night, but that special consideration had been given. That was a place I knew I could go. I was going to see Duke Ellington and Cab Calloway, and Jimmie Lunceford, and all of those great bands. They were going to come to Detroit. The parks were integrated. Eastwood Garden, which was an amusement park, was not segregated. Most of the parks in all of the cities were segregated, but not in Detroit. Belleville High, which was a place where you would go in Detroit to swim and spend your day. Right across the river is Windsor, Canada, and on this side is Detroit. All places were integrated. So Detroit turned out to be just a wonderful city. Besides the school, I went to what was one of the greatest music schools in the world. The head of the music department was Doctor Clarence Burn, whose son was my classmate, and joined Jimmy Dorsey's orchestra at the age of sixteen or seventeen. It was in [the] encyclopedia of jazz. They'll have it right there. He replaced Tommy Dorsey (they were the Dorsey Brothers). This was when they were splitting up. So it was some school. This guy, he could already play everything that Tommy Dorsey played. Not only that, his two sons could play every instrument in the band—could actually perform on it and could write music. Bobby of course joined Jimmy. He became a star with Jimmy Dorsey's band, and then got his own band. His brother also joined Jimmy Dorsey too. Also coming out of there would be people like Sam Donahue. I don't know if you ever heard of Sam Donahue, but he was a fine white tenor player who also joined Jimmy Dorsey but then got his own orchestra. Sonny Burke was from Detroit. I know you know who Sonny Burke is. So Detroit was really an outstanding place to be. They had many bands in the city. I played with a lot of bands there. I played with Gloster Current's band (doesn't mean anything to you). But Gloster Current was already a fine musician . . . played sax . . . could write and arrange . . . had the most popular band (young band) in Detroit. I finally got in his band and he later became the executive secretary of the NAACP and remained that until way up into the sixties because he was out here when I played the Image Awards, which is a thing that they have every year in the NAACP. He came out that year. But this guy became the executive secretary in the NAACP. So it was a great time to really be around musicians like that.

I finally ended up in the best band in Detroit. They called it the best band because it was the oldest band and had the best job. It was with Cecil Lee's band. I have pictures of everything to show that. Some of the fine guys that were there, they had played in McKinney's Cotton Pickers band. The Chocolate Dandies . . . in the other big orchestras from around the country. It was good to get in this band because (I was still in school at that time) . . . I met so many great people . . . Billy Eckstine, a girl who later became his wife, June Eckstine . . . he met her there. Bill Bailey, the great dancer, Pearl Bailey's brother. I met Pearl there. Of course, they had to hire her if they wanted Bill to do any of the work. She was an entertainer. And I met many people in the business that I would meet later, that would be able to help me. Also Jimmie Lunceford came over to our school as did the Dorsey brothers. In fact, whenever the big bands would come into the theater, Michigan Theatre, the Fox Theatre . . . whatever theater they were playing in, they would come over to the school. So I got a chance to meet Jimmie Lunceford. I never thought I'd be in his band. That came later. But I spent a little time there with the guys at the Plantation Club Orchestra and learned a lot because these guys were really top-notch musicians. So I was learning a lot by meeting musicians like that. Later on, after I spent a few years with them, I realized I had to move on because I wanted to get into the mainstream of what was happening in jazz. And I had read about Chick Carter's band. Chick Carter was a singer who had worked at this club, but he later organized a band. Snooky Young was a member of that band. And I read in the paper they had just come from New York at the Apollo Theater. So I said, "Now I want to be with some guys like that and I want to get moving."

I got a job with Milt Buckner . . . Milt Buckner was a great writer and his brother [Ted] was a great sax player who played with Jimmie Lunceford. Milt played with Lionel Hampton, he wrote "Hamp's Boogie Woogie." He wrote many of the big great arrangements. They knew me [and my trumpet playing] because I played in these other bands in Detroit. And I got this job at the Plantation because Milt had written an arrangement. He had a G in it and he said, "If you can play this one, you've got the job." And I played it and I got the job. So [my high note trumpet playing since Memphis] helped me quite a bit.

Now, in the meantime, I've already met Dizzy Gillespie. We would become friends. He stayed there about eight weeks with Edgar Hayes's band. Barry Harris, I had already met him. He's the guy that played with Charlie Parker's Quintet. He's the guy that co-authored "Ornithology." So I knew all of them in the Jimmie Lunceford band. Sy Oliver would take me and then put his chair up at the Graystone Ballroom and said, "You just sit here beside me." And I'd sit there and Jimmie, of course, would be directing . . . I wasn't playing anything in the band, but Sy would just take me. He was one of my idols. And I got his job. I replaced him. The club that I worked at was called the Plantation Club. This was a club like the New York Cotton Club. Like the St. Louis Plantation. Like the Cincinnati Cotton Club. These places were all over the country. These were black nightclubs that were in the black neighborhood. But blacks couldn't go there. They couldn't attend these clubs, except in Detroit. Detroit was always different. It had a special show every week. They had that special time to come in and see the show each and every . . . and then boom! But, in these other places, they couldn't go. . . .

The shows were all black, the musicians all black . . . The owners were white. So we were going to go out. We had been in the Plantation for months and months . . . a matter of fact, it ran into years actually. And we were going to move to a club called the Billy D. Edgar Hayes's band replaced us and Dizzy Gillespie played in Edgar Hayes's band. We'd all hang out. You see this club was in the basement of a black hotel. The Norwood Hotel. Nice hotel. They had everything. So we'd hang out there all day. So, as I already mentioned, I met Dizzy right away. We were trumpet players. We'd talk. We became friends. He knew I was starting to write. He knew I was playing with this band. So we became friends. I'd see him every day. We'd talk music and hang out together. So that was in 1938.

CHAPTER 3

NEW YORK, JIMMIE LUNCEFORD, THE GREAT LAKES, AND THE FIRST GERALD WILSON ORCHESTRA

Reading a great deal of old jazz criticism is usually like boning up on the social and cultural malaise that characterizes and delineates the bourgeois philistine in America.
—LEROI JONES (AMIRI BARAKA)

Wilson's journey to New York actually started during his tenure with Cecil Lee's Plantation Club band in Detroit. He recalled the transitions.

Wilson: That change is going from the Plantation Club band where we bring in Billy Eckstine. Billy Eckstine came to sing in Detroit in 1938. He met his wife there. He met her in Detroit. She was in the show. He wanted to learn how to play the trumpet. He didn't have a trumpet. I had two trumpets. I said, "Here, you can take my trumpet. You can take this one as long as you are here and use it." Which he did. The guy was a very talented guy. By the time he got his own band, he could play some fine solos on the trumpet. Then he picked up the valve trombone and played it. After that, he picked up the guitar. So we were great friends, Billy Eckstine and myself. He was there before he joined Earl Hines. He followed Herb Jeffries. Of course, Jeffries had left before then. I knew Herb before that. He left Detroit to join Earl Hines. Then he left to join Duke. Then Eckstine joined Earl Hines. He was from Detroit.

    Yeah, so that's the one we want to build on. The Plantation Club band to Lunceford. How I ended up there. I actually spent two years with the

Plantation Club band. I've got pictures from them. I was still in school. I was still going to high school. They used to call me "school boy." Of course, girls, they'd come and I'd be back there, studying. They'd call me "blood," "young blood." So those were the days. I was able to learn a lot. They had good arrangers in the band. They were giving me pointers on how to do things. So I was learning from both ends . . . from school and by playing in this band. As I said, after two years of that, I wanted to move on. So I got this chance to join Chick Carter's band. Chick Carter was playing in Saginaw, Michigan. The job was supposed to be for three weeks. It ended up being for three days. In other words, I joined it over the weekend. I played Friday, Saturday, and Sunday, and that was the end of the job. We came back to Detroit for a week. They had a job in Flint. We went back to Flint. I played Flint with the Chick Carter band and then it was over. They had one more job. I didn't know that at the time. So Snooky Young and Mitchell Woods later played with Count Basie and Duke Ellington. They told me, "Come on and go to Dayton and stay with us." So I went to Dayton and while I was in Dayton . . . we were battling Erskine Hawkins on that job. So I knew all the guys in Erskine Hawkins's band, and my dear friend there was Sammy Lowe, who was the top arranger in the band and the lead trumpet player. That day I had received a wire from Jimmy Lunceford inviting me to join his band. So Sammy had heard about it and he said to me, "Gerald, I heard you got a wire from Jimmie Lunceford to join their band." I said, "Yeah." He said, "Are you going to join?" I said, "No, I'm going to stay with this band. I like this band. It's a good band." It was a good band. He said, "Look this band is breaking up tonight. This is the last job." So then I went over and asked some of the guys in the band, and Ray Perry, who was a fine sax player and played violin and clarinet . . . he was leaving to go right home to Boston. He later went right on with Lionel Hampton's band. Harpo, another trombone player in the band, he went home. But then he went on to join Lionel Hampton also.

So then I called the number that was on the telegram, and I talked to Jimmie Lunceford. And he said go down to the train station because the Western Union had a place in the train station. "You'll have a ticket and some money to come to New York." And that was the next morning. I did exactly that. And things were beginning to change then, because, the first thing I did was when Eddie Tompkins met me, he said, "First we got to stop at the tailor downstairs so they can measure you up for your uniform." Seven different uniforms! We went on. He took me over to where I was going to stay that night. I stayed over at the YMCA. This is really like heaven now. I mean, New York City now and I'm joining Jimmie Lunceford's band. They were staying at the Y. That's where they would leave from. On 135th Street and Seventh Avenue and right across the street is Small's Paradise, which was one of the big nightclubs at the time. And so I'm really in heaven. We leave the next night on a tour and Sy is still in the band. Sy is playing out his two-week notice. He would leave to join Tommy Dorsey. Now, remember this is the same guy who took me and sat me beside him. I knew all the members of the band. So I was very lucky to join this band. And what made it so good for me . . . the band was at the height of its success. They were going to reach their prime. So they could still play all of the same numbers that they were playing . . . all of the hit records. Of course, we could play all of that. I sang in the quartet. I sang in the trio. I could do all of that. I didn't play for two weeks until my uniforms came and we got to Cleveland, Ohio. That would be the first night that I would play in the band . . . which was a great night too by the way, because the band was playing and Sy was sitting there. I read everything and kept on and Sy said, "If you read this number, I'm going to give you five dollars," which was a lot of money. So this was a tough one. But what he didn't know was that I knew the number real well anyway. But the band was happy. And then they'd always test you out. They would test you out on "Stardust." We got to play "Stardust" that night and Jimmie Lunceford said, "Play the solo." So I stood up and played. I'd been playing "Stardust" since before I left Memphis. That was it. But I got to think that it was because of the fact that Sy was leaving to join Tommy Dorsey, that I got this job. So I got Tommy Dorsey to thank for hiring Sy or else I might not have gotten that job.

So when I joined Jimmie Lunceford in 1939, it was Dizzy Gillespie who came and took me and said, "I am going to show you the ropes around New York. First I'm going to take you over to place called Mrs. Collins's. Anytime you don't have any money or anything, you can come here. You can get anything you want. If you've got to have a room, Mrs. Collins has got a room for you. You don't have to pay in advance." You have somebody vouching for you. So he was a friend. Actually we became really good friends.

Dizzy didn't go to Cab Calloway until the 1940s. So at this time he would be playing with Lucky Millinder and us. By the way, of course, this was the time when guys were jamming all the time and jamming up at Milton's. He played with Teddy Hill's band. Teddy Hill was a big man. He was an old guy that actually got things started up at Milton's because many of the great players played with Teddy Hill's band. Chu Berry played with Teddy Hill's band. Roy Eldridge, who was taking over from Louis Armstrong. He was the top trumpet player in the world. So they all played with Teddy. Chick Webb's band was still going. They had great musicians like Edgar Sampson . . . all these guys. All of these musicians are there and you see them there. I'd see Coleman Hawkins and Ben Webster. Duke's in town. I mean, these are all the kinds of friends. Me joining the Lunceford band, I'm joining one of the top ten bands in the country.

I stayed with Lunceford's band for three years. We would play in all the big places, but we still couldn't stay in the hotels all over the country. Some of them we could. Like Boston was one of the places that was pretty good. Montreal. Toronto. Then we played the Sherman House in Chicago. Of course, we didn't stay there, though. We played there six weeks. They started hiring black bands. Jimmie Lunceford's band is also the first black band to play the Paramount Theatre in New York City. The Lunceford band was so popular. You wouldn't believe it. They could outdraw any of the bands.

This was 1939, 1940, 1941, and 1942. And many things changed during that period. The Lunceford band got better. Everybody was wanting . . . see, it was six months later that Snooky was able to join the band because Eddie Tompkins went into the service. But, they could still play all the music that they played. Plus, he didn't hire me as an arranger, although I did some arranging at the time. My first two numbers were recorded in 1940 and one in 1941. He hired a guy named William Moore, who was one hell of a writer. And he wrote a whole bunch of stuff. When I played for him, it was like no other band in the world! And the band skyrocketed. We did all kinds of things. Very visual. We made [the film] *Blues in the Night* here [in Los Angeles] with Warner Brothers in 1941. We played the Casa Mañana in Culver City in 1940. We played the Paramount downtown. We played everywhere and would draw so many people you couldn't get in. [We toured] every state in the Union, except the Dakotas. But we passed through the Dakotas. We were coming to the top, to Iowa from Chicago.

We'd go through Iowa then to Minneapolis. We crossed the top on over to Seattle.

I joined [Lunceford] in 1939. In 1940, we were to tour Europe. We'd be gone six weeks. They had been there before. We were in the Paramount Theatre in New York City. And on the day that we were to leave, that night . . . we all had our bags. We had little trunks for our personal clothes, but we had big trunks for the uniforms. But we received this letter from the State Department that we wouldn't be able to leave because there was a war. So to show you how powerful the Lunceford band is . . . two weeks off and we were already booked all over the country. We started touring all over the country. Again. We were back out to Hollywood. We made *Blues in the Night* in 1941. And if you hear the band . . . Have you ever seen that movie? I'll show it to you sometime. You should hear the band. The band is like . . . the band is powerful.

It was during this time that Wilson started doing more arranging.

Wilson: I did my first . . . It wasn't what they wanted. And it wasn't that bad but it wasn't what they wanted. And then I made my next arrangement in 1940. It's called "Hi Spook" and it became a big hit. Then the next year, in '41, I did "Yard Dog Mazurka." That's the number that Stan Kenton used for that theme. That progression had never been used in jazz before. Also the one I used in "Hi Spook" had never been used before. I play that right now. It's like . . . I played it in Chicago about a month ago. It was just ahead of its time. That was "Yard Dog Mazurka." But it wasn't Kenton. Everybody says it was Kenton that took "Yard Dog Mazurka," but it was his band. Pete Rugolo arranged it, but the guy that made up the song the way they made it up . . . first of all, you got to know that you're using this progression . . . so he was a trumpet player. His name was Ray Wetzel. I knew Ray. I got a little angry the first time I heard it. I heard a little "Intermission Riff." I said, "That's my number." And then I had a lawyer friend of mine, he's still here by the way. Of course, he was the one . . . he was part of the [Musicians' Union] amalgamation when we wanted to move, found out what to do. I'm the one who actually put in the first motion that there would be a special meeting called for the specific purpose of amalgamating [the segregated African American] Local 767 and Local 47 [in which blacks were not permitted membership]. I got it from this lawyer who was a friend of mine in Detroit when I was going to school. So I went to him. I said, "Man, this guy took my number." He said, "Gerald, the copyright laws . . . he would have to take all of eight bars for you to do anything." They didn't do that. They took less. And then at the end they just changed it. So at that time they had to take eight bars. And so he told me, "There's nothing you can do about it."

I asked Wilson if Wetzel knew what he had done.

Wilson: Oh, he knew it! They all knew it! Pete Rugolo and I are good friends. They knew what they were doing and there was no law against it. Of course, I was really angry for a while. But anyway those were my first numbers. And then later I had others.

TO CALIFORNIA

I asked Wilson why he left the Lunceford band.

Wilson: I was going to go into the service. I was 1-A, so I knew I was going to go into the service. And I moved out to California. I always said I was going to move to California. So I came out and said, "Well, I'll go into the service from California." So I came out here. But I stayed out of the service for about a year. So I played in between that time. I played with the Les Hite band. I wrote for them. And they had a good band, by the way. Dizzy Gillespie had played with them. And Joe Fuller had played with them. In fact, I talked with them before I left Lunceford. And then they did good.

Snooky Young came out. Now, Snooky and I left [Jimmie Lunceford] the same night. He was 1-A too. He never did go in the service but he came out to join Lester Young and Leon's group. But he didn't like playing in small groups. So he came over by Les Hite's rehearsal. We were getting ready to do this tour. And he said, "I'm going with you guys." Then we came back and we played all that stuff. Les Hite formed his band . . . he was based here [in Los Angeles]. He was a very popular man back in the thirties here. He played at Sebastian's Cotton Club. We didn't play there with him. But he had already been to New York with his band.

[Also in the band were] Walter Williams and Jack Trainer. Jack Trainer was a trumpet player. He had been with Lionel Hampton. We played with them and toured with Les Hite. We toured with Les Hite up the coast all the way to Vancouver. We played theaters in San Francisco and Oakland. We played in Oregon. We played in Washington state, in Seattle and Olympia. We played in Grand Falls. Even in Montana. And finally we went on into Vancouver, where we played the Beacon Theatre there where all of the bands played. And then we returned to Los Angeles. And on the return to Los Angeles, we did an engagement at the Louisiana Club which was on Wilshire Boulevard in what section is now called the "Miracle Mile." We played eight weeks there. That was a memorable time because Buddy Colette was a member of the band. Charles Mingus was a member of the band. It was a very good band, by the way. And we played the Coca-Cola broadcast. You know, Coca-Cola had a thing every year where they would send bands all around to play for the armed services. We traveled to Fort Huachuca to play that Coca-Cola broadcast. And then we also returned back here to Los Angeles. It wasn't too long after that, that Les Hite disbanded the band.

And at that time I was able to talk with Benny Carter . . . [he] had been in town [Los Angeles]. Benny Carter had already been with his band in New York. So I knew Benny. So Benny called me and wanted me to join his band. So I said, "Well, Benny, listen" . . . I knew Benny was having a little trouble in his band getting guys . . . I said, "Listen, I can bring you a whole trumpet section [from the Les Hite band]." He said, "Yeah?" I brought in this trumpet section. They could play anything he had. J. J. Johnson was in the band . . . Bump Meyers . . . We could play any kind of music you had. We're going to play it perfect any time and we did. He was thrilled to death. This trumpet section also played in the movie for Warner Brothers, *This Is the Army.* They had the Cotton Club Boys come on to do their act. We played all the music with a sixty-five-piece orchestra and just these four black trumpet players. So I could tell you how good the trumpet section was. We played all the stuff at MGM. We just had a field day. Jack Trainer, who had been with Lionel Hampton. Walter Williams, who had been with Lionel Hampton. And Les Hite, Snooky, and myself. This trumpet section was so good . . . like the night when we opened with them on Santa Monica Boulevard. We were playing at the Hollywood Cafe. We'd just play all the toughest music like it was nothing. Benny was so happy.

While we were with Benny Carter there, Snooky Young and the trumpet section plus J. J. Johnson . . . we were also doing extra work around town during that period with Phil Moore, an outstanding arranger and composer who was doing special shows at CBS over on Sunset Boulevard under Meredith Willson, the one who wrote [the Broadway musical and eventual film] *The Music Man*. And we would do these shows every week on CBS. So, that was a time to also do some writing. Of course, I did some writing and J. J. Johnson was also a fine writer. So, some good things happened right in there.

With Snooky Young, I was able to see Tommy Dorsey's band at the Palladium here [in Los Angeles]. And Sy had invited both of us to come see him. Snooky and I, we were with Benny Carter's band at that time. We were a different kind of people. I said, "Look, why don't we go and buy a ticket?" We went up to the box office. The young lady said, "We can't sell you a ticket." I said, "Why, why can't you sell us a ticket?" We just kept insisting until she got a little frustrated about it. I said, "Well, why don't you call the manager?" The manager came over. The guy said, "No, I can't sell you a ticket." He looked at us and I said, "Why can't you sell us a ticket?" He said, "Well, you have on a zoot suit." I said, "What's a zoot suit?" He said, "Well, it's the one with the small cuffs." Sy Oliver said, "Where've you guys been? I've been waiting for you!" We were standing down there in the front looking at the band like everybody else. But we didn't always do that there. We started going in Sternberger's, which is right across the street from where the Union is now. It was a white restaurant. One night, Snooky and I went there. We just walked on in there.

I asked Wilson some questions about this incident.

Loza: So in other words, the Palladium . . . was it also a racial thing then?
Wilson: Yes. No blacks could ever play there.
Loza: When they let you in, you were the only blacks there?
Wilson: We were the only blacks!
Loza: But they were using the zoot suits as an excuse.

Wilson: That's the excuse they were using then. I doubt anybody else tried. Of course, it was many years later . . . it wouldn't be until the late fifties that they started renting it out for special dances.

Wilson commented that the incident at the Palladium occurred during the 1940s. He continued to discuss the race issue and the gradual integration that began to develop in some of the big bands.

Wilson: Sy Oliver, being a black musician, became the chief guy there. Blacks had already integrated bands years ago. Charlie Barnett had like five blacks at one time. Benny Goodman, three. Roy Eldridge joined and then broke the line. First of all, Gene Krupa actually broke the line of the blacks sitting up there, in the band. That was with Roy Eldridge. And Charlie Shavers became the lead trumpet for Tommy Dorsey. He stayed with him for years. So we were doing that all the time. We would just walk into a place.
Loza: To challenge them.
Wilson: Yeah. It was the Redwood Inn down on Eighth and Western . . . all of a sudden, one night, a gang of us guys finished a dance and said, "Let's go in here." And we just walked on in there. And for many it was like, when you open the door and walked in . . . silence. Complete silence. And then back on to eating.

With Benny Carter we [also] did a kind of a trip up to San Francisco. We played the Orpheum Theatre there with Benny Carter and along with Catherine Dunham and her dancers. And also Ethyl Waters who was a big star at that time. We had quite a few nice things with Benny Carter. We were in the movie *Thousands Cheer* back with Lena Home where we were both seen and heard. I later of course was also seen and heard with Benny in [the Hollywood film] *An American in Paris* as a trumpet player (it was a smaller group, though). Anyway, I stayed with Benny. We played jobs around town. We played the Hollywood Club, which was on Santa Monica Boulevard. And also we played out in Hermosa Beach at Zucca's Terrace. This was a place where they had bands. Johnny Richards was one of the bands that played there. And the fine young Mexican singer that made "Green Eyes" at that time was a drummer, I believe, with Johnny Richards . . . Andy Russell. We played there at Zucca's Terrace and it was there that I was inducted into the service.

THE NAVY BAND

Wilson: I got my notice to report to the armed services. It was a good time. One thing that happened here, Steve, was that the fellow that replaced me with the Jimmie Lunceford band . . . his name was Freddy Webster. He replaced me in April of 1942. He replaced me but he didn't stay long because he was out on the coast and he joined Benny Carter's band, the band that I was playing with there. They took me down to the induction place to get inducted. And that was when I found out that no matter where I was inducted, I was to go to Great Lakes, Illinois. I would go in the ship's company band there along with Willie Smith who had been the lead alto with Jimmie Lunceford. Clark Terry, a great trumpet player, was also in that band. Many other fine musicians from all over the country. They had actually handpicked these guys and it was really a great time because all I had to do was write music all day. So it was a good time to get a lot of work and a lot of studying done. I was very fortunate at that time to be able to do a lot of experimenting. I'm moving ahead and forgetting things. I'm going to take a curve back.

[And as I said,] I'm already set because Willie Smith is already in the Navy. That's the first lead alto man with Jimmie Lunceford and the man that, actually, everybody played for him. See, when you played in the Jimmie Lunceford band you didn't play for Jimmie Lunceford. You played for Willie Smith. Of course, Willie Smith doesn't miss anything. And besides, he's avant-garde on his horn. He's not like Benny Carter. He's avant-garde. In his solos, you hear that he's in another world. And they'd just started taking the first Marines too (the first blacks in the Marines). By the way, we were the first blacks in the Navy. I was to go to Great Lakes, Illinois. That's exactly what happened. I was in Sixth Company Band. And we had such a band you wouldn't believe . . . a fabulous band. And it was a great time because all I had to do was write and play. You could experiment with anything you wanted to. We lived in the city, Chicago. I never slept a night on the base.

I had a good time trying to hone my craft. Having my own style going for me at that time, they played a lot of my arrangements and I did a lot of arrangements. And it was a good time that I could do anything I wanted. They had all of the instruments that you needed. The band was very good. We played with all of the big acts that would come out to entertain. A group like Stuff Smith . . . I remember them coming through. They had Jimmy Jones with them, a fine pianist who later became Sarah Vaughan's accompanist and also who later worked for Duke Ellington. Also people like Lena Horne came out to entertain the soldiers. But also every Saturday night we would travel to Chicago to broadcast over at WBBM, a CBS station. So it was a good time because half of you had original numbers and they wanted as many original numbers that they could get so that there wouldn't be a problem clearing them for broadcast. Also, it was a good time to see things that were going on in Chicago and we could see things that I didn't understand. I often wondered why it was that there was never a black band to play at the Aragon. There never was a time that a black band played at the Aragon. At that time the Aragon was featuring a band on the weekend by the name of Lawrence Welk. So we know what later happened to Lawrence Welk [Welk became a major television start with his orchestra]. But never did any of the black bands ever play any one of those ballrooms, which, all I'm saying is that there were still so many racial things going on even in the big city of Chicago. And although we were in the Navy, it was also segregated. This would be the first time that there would be any black sailors ever. They had blacks working as mess boys, but they were just there to serve the officers. Although we were segregated, this . . . would be a time when we would have the first officers ever in the United States because they were training them to become officers. In fact, couple of the officers that were in my company during boot camp, later became the first officers ever in the United States.

Loza: But the bands were segregated?

Wilson: The bands were segregated.

Loza: Boot camp was all black?

Wilson: Boot camp was all black.

Loza: Your division was all black?

Wilson: All black.

Loza: Your superior officers?

Wilson: Yes.

Loza: The director of the band?

Wilson: The director of the band was black but he was under a white director also. There was a white director over him who might come in and conduct the orchestra. For instance, in our band (and I could tell you a little incident here) . . . Chief Oakes was his name. He was over a fellow by the name of Len Bowden, who was the black director. After I came in (I was one of the writers), Chief Oakes came up to me and he handed me a little piece of paper that had some music on it and he explained to me that this was a number that he had written for his wife and he would like me to take a look at it. So when I got to the barracks after I had finished talking with Chief Oakes, all of the other arrangers there (who were some nice arrangers) all laughed and said, "The Chief gave you that little piece of paper with music for his wife." They were making a joke of it. And I said, "Yeah, that's what it is." So I decided that I would make this number one of the biggest numbers in the repertoire. And I did. I worked on it and I made it up to be a star number in our shows. And the Chief loved it so much that the Chief explained to everybody that, "You just leave Wilson alone. He does whatever he wants to do here. If he wants to go do something and if he doesn't, he doesn't have to go." So he was very well taken with this number because I had written it and did a good job.

Loza: That was a pretty smart move.

Wilson: Well, I just felt bad that these guys would make fun of him. So even after that we had some of the best writers there. One guy, a good friend of mine from Los Angeles, later worked with Elvis Presley. He was Elvis Presley's piano player and arranger. His name was Dudley Brooks. So he decided to do a fine, kind of a military version of this same number. And another guy who did vocal arrangements (we had so many people in the music department) later worked with Duke. On one of his shows he did a whole big octet thing for the band to sing. So then we put all three of these numbers together. They would end with mine. It started with the military. They would do the singing thing and then it would end with mine. This became one of the biggest numbers of the show, so after that they were no longer laughing at this number. One other incident is funny also. The [officer] who was over us . . . you know, in the Navy you have to go and swim every two or three days. I liked to swim. But you get tired of that. This [officer] also had a number he had written for his wife. So he gave it to me. I took it and I wrote it up for the band. And, of course, after that I never had to go swim anymore. So it was a nice time. I had some good things going there. It was a time that I could really study and hone my craft. I got a lot of numbers in on the broadcast. I was in the Navy in 1943 and 1944. When I was actually inducted into the Navy, I had a very serious sinus problem. They were experimenting with guys who had sinus problems. They had a thing where they would stick needles up your nose. So anyway, I had a few attacks of the sinus problem so they sent me to the hospital. And it was there that the doctor explained to me, "Well, Wilson, you have a very bad case of this. We are going to treat you. We don't know how this is going to work." It did pretty good but even after it was over, I was given a medical discharge from the Navy. So then I came out and that was near the end of 1944 and I returned to Los Angeles.

The actual name of the base was the Great Lakes Naval Training Station. What we did too other than that, we played for colors and to entertain the troops. We also formed bands to go to other bases. In fact, the guy that I played with in Detroit, he left as one of the leaders taking the band to, I think it was Alaska. We had a big jazz band. We had military bands that played the colors and marches, marching bands. Concert bands. We played everything. These musicians were all handpicked. So it was very nice. It was a chance to really expand upon musical talent. If you go in there with the right idea. You know, I was married at that time. I had married while I was still with the Jimmie Lunceford band . . . My first wife was a member of the Dandridge Sisters. So I'm kind of going back. You know, Dorothy Dandridge and her sister . . . there were two that were sisters. The other girl that sang in the trio was not a sister. These girls, Vivian and Dorothy, were the sisters, they had already sang in the Cotton Club, already been to Europe . . . they had already been to South America. They had already been to Hawaii. They were fine singers. We recorded them. We later took them on a tour with us, the Jimmie Lunceford band. They were fine singers. They could sing good and they were very entertaining. I married the girl that wasn't the sister. [Her name was Etta Jones.] So I was already married at the time when I was in the Navy. We later divorced. It lasted a while. It was nice. She had a nice family. It was a nice marriage. It was just that I was traveling with my own band and things happened later on. You know how those things happen.

BACK TO LA

Wilson: I returned to Los Angeles and I formed my own orchestra. At the time, I wasn't forming it to be my orchestra. I'd always planned to have a band. But Herb Jeffries, the singer that sang with Duke and Earl Hines, he was going to front this band. We were going to open up down on First and Los Angeles Street at a place called Shepp's Playhouse. Well, something happened just before we were to open and Herb took another job and left town. So the guy that owned the club told me, "You've got the band." And I opened up there. I played this big club down on First and Los Angeles. Right where the New Otani Hotel is sitting today. That's where it was. Blacks had just taken this club, although anybody could go in there. It wasn't a segregated club. I played downstairs in this big place that had a dance floor and where the big show was. There were chorus girls, acts, singers. Then, upstairs, Eddie Haywood's band played. There was a lounge and a bar where people could go. His band was really hot at that time. He had hit records going from "Begin the Beguine" to other hits at that time. So that was a nice time. I played there. I made my first stint at the Orpheum Theatre in 1945. And as soon as I finished there, I went to Salt Lake City for thirteen weeks at the biggest club in Salt Lake City. I had played there with Jimmie Lunceford's band two or three times before. I also played up in Idaho. I played Boise, Idaho, for a couple of weeks and then right back into Los Angeles. Back into this club. I also had another stint at the Orpheum Theatre, where I was the headliner this time. Eddie Haywood was the headliner the first time. One of the supporting acts that I had on my show was the Will Mastin Trio featuring Sammy Davis Jr. [This was] the Gerald Wilson Orchestra. I have pictures of the marquees and everything . . . I played a few other arrangements, but the bulk of everything was mine . . . At the first time, I didn't even bother to have a singer. They had somebody singing in the show, so I didn't need a singer. I picked up a singer, in fact, a guy that had been singing for Benny Carter. He was a good singer. His name was Dick Gray. He went up to Salt Lake with us.

In Salt Lake City (1945), was an all-white audience. They were a little . . . they had a special place in the club. These were people who were my guests. They could come and they would put them in this place. Jerry Jones, he knew me, and they'd book me back. We were so popular there. Some things happened there. This was a time when it was very segregated in Salt Lake City. We were staying at this hotel. And we were staying in a Chinese hotel downtown. And when we would go downtown to go to the movies when we first started there, they would start to tell us we could sit up in the balcony. And so after about a week or two we'd walk on down into this theater. And as I said, we were broadcasting over at NBC. So we got invitations from two or three other restaurants, "You are welcome here." And then the theaters started leaving us alone. They didn't bother us. Before we left there it had really turned out to be a fairly nice gig. We were so popular that after the first engagement we came to Los Angeles. We played in the theater. We went up to San Francisco and played the Brown Bomber Ballroom. That was a new ballroom in San Francisco. It later became the Primalon, which was a big ballroom on Fillmore. So we were booked back to Salt Lake City, but my booking agent got a better deal for me with Covy's Coconut Grove which was the world's largest ballroom in Salt Lake City. So it was there before Jerry Jones. You could just drive the bus right into the ballroom right in back of the bandstand. It was called Covy's Little America. He owned this big motel complex and he had booked our band in his place. Jerry Jones got very angry at me for going into this place because he had brought me there and now I went with this big guy. Covy was a big man, and in fact, if you go to Salt Lake City today, you'll find Covy's Little America is still a big thing. [Jerry Jones] was a promoter. His place was called the Rendezvous. Jerry Jones's Rendezvous. But I played there with Jimmie Lunceford when he was building it. In fact, the bandstand was rickety. It had boards all over it. When I went to play in it, it was now a plush little nightclub. Then he later bought Covy's Coconut Grove. I went back [to play there later] with Count Basie's band.

Loza: Now, these were all white establishments then? White owners too?

Wilson: Yeah. . . .

Loza: Mostly white audiences. Well, Salt Lake City, there were probably very few blacks at that time. There also was the Mormon Center.

Wilson: The Mormon Center was right up the street. We lived down near the railroad station from the Mormon temple. At that time they were really strange with you.

Loza: Now, did the Mormons go to your performances?

Wilson: I'm sure many of those people came in there. This place would be packed every night.

Loza: But what I meant was that I'm not sure if the Mormons dance or not. I was just wondering if . . . maybe they do dance. I was just wondering if . . . at that time of course, there was racism. In the Mormon religion, at that time of course, blacks were not permitted to be part of their religious orders. So it would just be an interesting face-off. An interesting encounter there in Salt Lake City, to imagine your band, mostly all black, in a city that had very few black inhabitants and on top of that was largely controlled by the Mormon religion, where being black was even not permitted in terms of being one of their priests or religious members. It demonstrates a fact that black music, jazz, which came out of the black tradition, was popular among everybody. In other words, they still figured out a way to sell it to everybody regardless of who was playing it, blacks or whites.

Wilson: Now, we could go to the railroad station. Of course, you know, now they have blacks in the Mormon Church.

Loza: Of course, most of the churches in the forties were segregated, even the other denominations.

Wilson: They were all segregated. Boise wasn't a bad place. We stayed at the white hotel. We played in a white ballroom. Of course, you didn't see any blacks in the town or in the city, but . . .

Loza: But you saw a lot of beautiful country.

Wilson: We had good engagements. It happened all the way up and down the coast in places like Olympia, Washington. You couldn't go in those places.

Loza: In Los Angeles, where your band was based, what many people have written about and documented was Central Avenue and African American culture. Was this already happening in the 1940s?

Wilson: Oh, yeah. I played up and down Central Avenue. I played the Elk's Auditorium. The Lincoln Theatre, I played there with Nat King Cole. I played the Club Alabam. I played the Downbeat Club. I played every place you could play on Central Avenue. My band was very popular. You have to remember, we played the Orpheum Theatre. We played in the Million Dollar. We played the Million Dollar with Jackie Robinson the baseball player. See, it was such a thing when this guy broke the color line in baseball. The first year, the minute the season was over, they booked him on a whole theater tour. All he would do is stand up there. A guy would come up and ask him questions . . . whatever city they go in. My band was the band chosen to back him. Later I became a good friend of his. I later even went to see him in New York after I joined Count Basie.

During this period, Gerald Wilson and his band prospered immensely, eventually performing a series of shows with vocalist jazz great Ella Fitzgerald. In Suite Memories, *a spoken word album and scrapbook produced by the MAMA Foundation (1996), Wilson recalled this high pinnacle period of his 1945–46 big-band show:*

My band was moving. I picked up a booker. The next thing I knew we were on our way to San Francisco where we played a couple of weeks at the Brown Bomber Ballroom, which was a ballroom named for Joe Lewis. It was a great success. We made a trip into St. Louis. We Played the Riviera. This is now '45. We went to Chicago that year. We had a little problem in Chicago with the union. In those days if you didn't file your contract two weeks before you got into town you were in trouble. I had a guy that was booking me but he didn't tell me this. So when we got to Chicago and were going to open up, the union came by and said, "We can't honor your contract. You did not file it the two weeks in advance." We had some bookings but there was about a five or six-week layoff. So we couldn't layoff in Chicago because we didn't have enough money to layoff around there. So while we were in Chicago, Eddie Rochester Anderson was on the Jack Benny show. He knew me. He liked my band and he was there at the Oriental and he sent for me. So I went down to the Oriental and Johnny Richards's band was backing him. He talked to me and said, "Hey, I hear you have a little problem here. The union wouldn't let you play." So he said, "I'll tell you what you can do, you go and get tickets for all of your men to go home and you stay here with me until the end of the engagement. And then you can go home after that. For me to do this for you, you're going to play a tour with me with your band." I said, "Fine that's great, I love it." What more could you ask. My band is going home to wait. I'm here. He's giving me plenty of money to enjoy myself. There was nothing to do but just relax. Well, anyway, I came back [to Los Angeles] and then revamped and started again. We played the Orpheum Theatre again. The tour began the night after we closed. We took off again. This time we went to Tucson. We had a string of army dates. We played Wichita Falls, Texas.

We played Mountain Home, Idaho. There was a big air base up there. Then we went to Colorado Springs. We stayed in the barracks there and played three things for them. We played Denver. We went back again through Texas on into Chicago and then to New York. We played the Apollo. It was very successful. We went directly from there to a ten-week engagement in Chicago and this is the way things happened.

The El Grotto was a fine [Chicago] nightclub where Fletcher Henderson played, Earl Hines played, Georgie Auld played (he followed me, actually). Stayed there ten weeks with my band. Had a great band there too. Right there I picked up a singer by the name of Joe Williams. While I was in Chicago though, big things happened before we left to go to St. Louis. Berle Adams of Mercury Records said, "Gerald, we would like for you to record for Mercury Records. A three-year contract. Your first date will be with Dinah Washington. This is not on your contract but this is just a bonus. You come and make this date with Dinah Washington with your band." Which I did. The dates are out now in CD. Dinah Washington and Gerald Wilson's orchestra. He was also the manager for Louis Jordan. Louis Jordan was the hottest thing in show business bar none. Duke Ellington, Count Basie, he could out draw them put together. At that time this was the most popular man in music. So for that thirteen weeks with him at the Paramount Theatre in New York City. These are contracts signed. I'm getting five thousand a week. Now in those days that's a lot of money. Five thousand a week is a lot of money. Plus, I'm booked to come back to the El Grotto for another ten weeks. I'm also booked to go back to the Apollo Theater. Schiffman is giving me two times a year. He knew me because I was a trumpet player with the Lunceford band. After we finished the engagement at the El Grotto, we go directly to St. Louis again. This time we were with Ella Fitzgerald. Ella Fitzgerald was the big star in my band. We played there six weeks and broke all records. And to show you how strong we were, they would have special nights where they would have battles and my band during our engagement there at that time, battled Ella Fitzgerald and Louis Armstrong put together. They teamed up and the battle was

Ella Fitzgerald and Louis Armstrong's orchestra and my band. Let me tell you we were tough.

My band at that time, we were into stuff that no one else was into. I had already introduced the augmented eleventh with the thirteenth to bands. No other band played that before I did. That's a harmonic structure that I was using in my band.

We were already playing bebop. My young players were all beboppers. Jimmy Bunn was one of the finest early young beboppers around. He's the piano player on "Lover Man" with Charlie Parker. Again, I had an integrated band. I had a young white trumpet player, whose name was Tommy Allison. He was a fine young bebop player. I had Benny Harris. Benny Harris of course was one of the early pioneers of bebop on trumpet. In fact he may have been one of the first bebop players because I had met him in Detroit when he came there with Lucky Millinder and his band. And he was already into some bebop. He's the guy that wrote "Ornithology" along with Charlie Parker. Anyway I had this fine band. I picked up another female too in Chicago. So I had two females in the band. A fine pianist named Vivian Fears who had played with Fletcher Henderson's band. And she wanted to play with our band because it was a very young band and we were a very exciting band. We had great arrangements and we were using things as I said that other people were not. For instance, we were doing "Out of This World" at that time. I reharmonized the structure for "Out of This World" for my band. I was using all alternate chords. In other words if the chord was B flat minor, I was using the alternative to that which would be D flat major. Everything was an alternate. And we had things like that going for us. My "Groovin' High." This is the record that I'm saying is the proof because it was recorded in 1945. My band was the most adventuresome band at that time. (Wilson 1996)

CHAPTER 4

MOMENT OF TRUTH

Only power that springs from the weakness of the oppressed
will be sufficiently strong to free both.
—PAULO FREIRE

In 1962, Gerald Wilson recorded an original blues piece titled "Moment of Truth," which was also the title track of one of his second Pacific Jazz Records LPs. The title and its meaning, however, could very easily have referred to a decision he made in St. Louis in 1946.

THE ST. LOUIS DECISION

Wilson: On the second trip with Ella Fitzgerald, and I haven't documented a thing about that weekend yet, but Ella Fitzgerald and I were a team. I played Chicago ten weeks in the biggest nightclub in Chicago. So my band being so popular, and all of a sudden, we'd already played the Apollo Theater by 1946. We'd been in New York. Philadelphia. Pittsburgh. And I was already booked to go thirteen weeks with Louis Jordan at the Paramount in New York, and it was then when I realized . . .

What Wilson realized was that he did not feel right. He was having a high-rolling success as a bandleader and arranger, leading and working with premier jazz artists of the day. But musically, artistically, he felt that he had not attained all of the technical skills or artistic diversity that

40

called to him as a composer. He wanted to study more. In Suite Memories
(Wilson 1996), Wilson recalled this moment of decision:

And there in St. Louis I realized that I had gotten to the top too
soon and I hadn't even started to do what I wanted to do. I needed
a lot more study and that was when I decided that I wasn't going
to take any of this because this isn't what I am looking for. When
I closed with Ella Fitzgerald I said, "I'm going home to study." And
of course everyone figured I was a nut including my booking agent
who wanted to kill me with all of these contracts that they had.
This wasn't what I was looking for. So I had to do the thing. I just
disbanded my band and said, "This is it." And I did.

*There was, however, one interruption that held up Wilson's sabbatical
just after he came home to Los Angeles.*

My phone rang, and who do you think it was on the phone? It was
Duke Ellington. He called me at my home and he wanted me to
do a couple of numbers for him. The Duke is a very suave man,
you know. Of course he really buttered me up. Like he would say,
"Mr. Wilson, one of the most illustrious writers today." You know
he's a man that has the words. And I was so glad to hear him call
because this was an opportunity I was waiting on. He said, "I've
got two numbers I need to record the day after tomorrow." This
was for Columbia Records. They were playing at the Casa Mañana
in Culver City. He said, "Can you write those numbers for me?"
I said, "Yes, and what are the numbers?" They were his numbers
"You've Got to Crawl Before You Walk" and "You're Just an Old
Antidisestablishmentarianismist" (Wilson 1996).

*Wilson would continue his artistic relationship with Duke Ellington and
through the years would work with him on a number of projects. These
included arrangements of "Perdido," "El Gato," and "Isle of Capri." He did
arrangements for Ellington for a Capitol Records date, and for an ap-
pearance at Disneyland, Ellington asked Wilson for some original pieces.
Wilson provided two compositions he had already arranged, "El Viti,"*

which with the Ellington band featured trumpeter Cat Anderson, and a "little rock and roll number" that Ellington was so impressed with that he suggested that Billy Strayhorn write lyrics for it. The piece, "Imagine My Frustration," with Strayhorn's newly penned lyrics, was eventually recorded on Verve Records by the Ellington Orchestra, featuring vocalist Ella Fitzgerald. Wilson recalled that a few years after this, jazz critic Leonard Feather called him to let him know that the same number was being performed in New York on Broadway in the hit musical Sophisticated Ladies.

Wilson also played trumpet on a number of Ellington's West Coast recordings or live concert dates. During Ellington's scoring and recording of the music track for Otto Preminger's classic film Anatomy of a Murder, Ellington relied on Wilson for both scoring pieces and playing one of the trumpet parts. Kirk Silsbee makes the point that "over many years of working with Ellington, Wilson made numerous important contributions to Ellington's orchestra which have remained an inextricable part of its repertoire" (Silsbee 1996: 10).

MUSICAL STUDY IN LOS ANGELES

During the period after he left Lunceford's band, occasional interruptions for outside work would occur, as had happened with Wilson's first call from Duke Ellington. But Wilson's main focus between the years 1946 and 1948 was one of seclusion and musical study. In order to support himself and his family, for a period he operated a grocery store in Los Angeles.

Wilson's long-range goals included preparing himself for scoring motion pictures, composing for symphony orchestra, and cultivating his skills as a composer and orchestrator. Thus, Wilson "woodshedded" during this period, studying and analyzing the works of composers such as Stravinsky, Falla, Ravel, Debussy, Bartók, Kabalevsky, Rodrigo, Beethoven, and Khachaturian. One of Wilson's major influences at this time was Phil Moore (previously discussed in chapter 3). Moore was both mentor and professional colleague to Wilson.

Phil Moore. He was a pianist. He was an arranger, a composer, and even an orchestrator. He was also Lena Horne's accompanist.

He also did a lot of work for many singers. But he could do it for everything. He was writing for MGM movies. I came here [Los Angeles] with Lunceford. I met him the first week I came here. He came out to bring an arrangement for the Jimmie Lunceford band to rehearse, and he wanted to sell it to them, which he did. And I was amazed at this orchestration, this arrangement . . . this composition. And right away I wanted to meet this man and be a friend of his. And he liked me too. He knew that I could write. We became very good friends. And when I left the Lunceford band I came out here and I worked on every record that he practically made with Lena Horne. In the movies with Lena Horne. Doing stuff with Lennie Hayden. And her recordings. Phil also was re-cording for the same guy that I later recorded for, Albert Marx on Discovery Records. He made many, many sides on Discovery Re-cords. Some featured Calvin Jackson, the great pianist. This would be with large orchestras. Thirty-five pieces, forty pieces. It would be a jazz orchestra or whatever. He did the trombone concerto that was written by Nathaniel Shilkret. He was a big man out here at MGM. And Phil did so much work out at MGM. It was Phil Moore who did the arrangements. You see, Duke Ellington, when they were making *Cabin in the Sky*, Duke had to leave. He couldn't finish up the picture. So at that time Barney Bigard had left Duke. Rex Stewart had left Duke. So you've got two great soloists here that were in the Duke Ellington Orchestra, and Phil Moore is the only man I know besides Billy Strayhorn that could write just like Duke Ellington if he wanted to. If he had to, he did. He finished the arrangements and the pieces and the people thought it was Duke Ellington's band. And this was a band he'd picked up around town. I was in the band. Lee Young, Lester's brother, was the drummer. Red Calendar was on bass. So Phil Moore was amazing. He's the guy that wrote "Shoo Shoo Baby," by the way, which was a huge pop hit. It went to the top of the Hit Parade. I played with this group, by the way. It was called Phil Moore and One More. I was the "One More." I was the trumpet player. He wanted me to go to New York with him to play at the Café Society where he played for many weeks. He later made his home in New York for a long time. He had his apartment in the Carnegie Hall building. That's where his apartment was and where it should be because he is truly one of the great musicians of our time. He turned me on to things that I had never been turned on to. I'd go to his home. We'd listen to Stravinsky's *Petrushka*. We'd listen to *The Firebird*. We'd listen to Khachaturian. We'd listen to Kabalevsky, Glière, Villa Lobos. You know . . . All kinds of modern composers. So Phil was one of my true mentors. (Wilson 1996)

INTERNSHIP WITH COUNT BASIE

In 1948, Wilson encountered another opportunity that would also have a lasting and meaningful impact on his musical career and philosophy.

In 1948 I received a call from Count Basie. He was playing at the Lincoln Theatre here [Los Angeles]. They were already into the engagement and he said, "Will you come down and play the last three days with us here?" Snooky Young, my dear friend Snooky, had just left the band. So I said, "Yes, I'll do that." . . . I went down. I played the three days and Count said, "Why don't you come and go as far as Chicago with us and by that time Snooky will be back." And I said, "OK, that would be nice." It was nice meeting Paul Gonsalves. Earl Warren was back in the band, a great lead alto man, and Jack Washington on the baritone. But anyway, I leave with the band. So we got to Chicago and I was anxious to get back to Los Angeles. Snooky didn't come so Basie said, "Gerald, can you stay? We're going into New York. We're getting ready to do a big show. We're going to have chorus girls. We're going to have different acts. It's going to be a big production. I want you to write an opening for the chorus girls." Ziggy Johnson would be the choreographer, one of the great ones of all time. I would write the middle number and the finale. Also they were getting ready to do their first Carnegie Hall concert. And he came to me and said, "Gerald, I want you to write me a suite." He loves to play poker. He likes to play poker and talk. In other words he liked to gamble no matter what. But he really loves poker. So he said, "I want you to write me a suite. I want five numbers in it. We're going to call it *The Royal Suite*.

This five numbers would be the ace of hearts, the king of hearts, the queen of hearts, the jack of hearts, and the ten of hearts. So I agreed to do this and do this right. Also he wanted me to write a new number for Clark Terry who was the new trumpeter in the band, so I did that. Also the singer in the band—his name was Bob Bailey. Bob of course lives right up in Las Vegas, of course he's the big man up there. Also he wanted me to do a remaking of a number that he had recorded years ago, "Swinging at the Daisy Chain" or something like that. So this is eight numbers. I had eight numbers on the Carnegie Hall concert. We rehearsed in all of the New York studios for it. The concert was very successful. The band was very good. They had some great players in that band. You must remember Paul Gonsalves was in that band. Buddy Tate was in that band. Earl Warren was back. See, "Q" (Quincy Jones) was there. Jack Washington was still there, the great baritone man. Dicky Wells, which I wrote a special number for him to play, was in *"The Royal Suite."* It was called "The Jack of Hearts." And it was a great band. Clark Terry, Sweets Edison of course. Sweets Edison, the giant of the trumpet as you know. Jimmy Nottingham. They had five trumpets in those days. The band, as I said, was really a roaring band. After that we had a great tour. We toured all over the country. We went to Florida, Tennessee, Kentucky, Illinois, Michigan, and Massachusetts. We'd have big shows with Billy Eckstine and the Nicholas Brothers, Count Basie's band at the Earle Theatre in Philadelphia with Sarah Vaughan, the Illinois Jaquet group that was very hot at that time. They were still doing "Robin's Nest" and things like that. So it was really a great time for the Basie band . . .

When I came back to New York, Basie was getting ready to record. He was going to be recording for Victor. So he wanted me to write all of the arrangements for the dates. So I was living at the Theresa at that time, and to make sure that I wrote my music for him and that I wouldn't be late or anything . . . he knew that at that time I was a young man and I liked to have a good time. I was out on the town in New York, loved New York City, still love New York City, it's a wonderful place. But he said, "Gerald, I think I better take you to my home. You'll stay at my home while you are writing this music." He lived in Saint Alban's and it was a great experience. Count Basie lived in one of the finest neighborhoods in Saint Alban's. And he had a wonderful house, beautiful furniture, everything right in place like it's supposed to be, including downstairs in the basement, he had a regular soda fountain. You could make your own sundae. You could make your own banana split. Go play the pinball machine. They had two or three pinball machines, which he liked to do anyway. And you know, tables and chairs. You'd go down and listen to the music. So it was a great time and a lot of fun with Count Basie. He was giving me the advantage of having a keyboard. He didn't have a piano in his house. He had a Hammond organ is his home.

Next door to Count Basie's home was a ravine. It was like, you can't go in there, it's like a little forest. It had vines and little trees. It's just there. And I told Count Basie . . . I said, "You know, last night I just heard this great number." I said, "I heard it all. I could hear the different creatures that live in the ravine." I could hear them. And he used to call me . . . he thought I was kind of nutty. He told all of his bands about it. But I did write the number up, by the way. I wrote up what I thought I heard that night. I was probably dreaming, but it became one of my biggest numbers. It's a number that I recorded called "Algerian Fantasy" and Basie always tells a story about that. He says, "Gerald heard this whole big symphonic number that night from the ravine." But I really did, you know? I heard the bass part over here and I would hear these things coming over here. It would be like there would be the flutes coming in, and I would hear these different creatures coming in and I was able to write the number like nothing. (Wilson 1996)

During his tenure with Count Basie, Wilson also composed what has become one of his classics, "You Better Believe It," in addition to "Jammin' in C" and the ballad "Katy" (named for Basie's wife), and co-composed with Basie "St. Louis Baby." Eventually, he would also pen one of his classic compositions/arrangements for Basie's band, "Blues for the Count." Doug Ramsey quotes Wilson describing his time and experiences with Basie as something akin to an internship: "That was study, too . . . sitting where swing really happened. That great rhythm section was really the common denominator for swing" (Ramsey 2000: 3).

THE ORCHESTRA AND INFLUENCE OF DIZZY GILLESPIE

As the Count Basie Orchestra disbanded in 1949 (although it would subse-quently reorganize), Wilson proceeded to join the Dizzy Gillespie big band. There, he performed alongside musicians such as Jimmy Heath, Paul Gonsalves, and John Coltrane, and contributed arrangements including "Taboo," "Dizzier and Dizzier," "Couldn't Love, Couldn't Cry," and the aforementioned "Katy." Doug Ramsey notes that while Wilson played in Gillespie's band, "he arranged 'Guachi Guaro,' which became influential in the development of Latin jazz in the '40s and had a second life when Cal Tjader adapted it in the '50s. During all of that extracurricular activity, Wilson continued studying and preparing for his next steps" (Ramsey 2000: 3). Gillespie, however, would always retain a special place in Wil-son's musical philosophy and historical perspective of jazz.

He changed his style and made that great transition from a Roy Eldridge-style man to bebop, and, of course, he must have been waiting for Charlie Parker to come and join him because he's the same as Charlie Parker. To my mind, Dizzy was here to give us all a message too, only he stayed around for a long time. He didn't leave. He stayed and he reaped the benefits of being a genius and being a messenger. I . . . wrote music for his band and I . . . played in his band. And we were always good friends. He would come to my home. He wouldn't come to Los Angeles without coming to my home. Dizzy Gillespie, in my mind, will be remembered for a lot of things. First of all I consider him one of the great innovators of all time. He's one of the founders of bebop. He was right there on the scene. There were a number of people involved with this, but he, of course, [was] one of the principal players; he will be remembered for the great style that he created on the trumpet for bebop. If you play modern trumpet you must play a lot of the things that Dizzy Gillespie actually created. I think that he'll be remembered as one of the greatest of all time." (Wilson 1996)

Like Basie's band, Dizzy's band also disbanded by 1950, due to the difficult and changing economics of that period for sustaining large orchestras in the jazz industry. That same year, 1950, Wilson was approached in New

York by Earle Dancer, who had been a producer at the Cotton Club, about
doing a southern tour with Billie Holiday. Wilson then met with Billie
Holiday's manager, John Levy, to assemble a big band to back her for a
tour (see Clarke 2000).

> Well this was just something that's like dropping out of the sky,
> a wish that probably I never wished it, but I would have if I had
> thought about it. And I immediately said, "Yes." All I had to do was
> send home [Los Angeles] for my trunks of music and I had plenty
> of music to play. And we would go to Philadelphia and put a band
> together. Incidentally, we had some fine members of the band . . .
> First of all, Philly Jo Jones was our drummer, and one of our trum-
> peters was Johnny Coles, one of the great jazz players. Willie Cook,
> the great lead player that played with Earl Hines, played with Duke
> Ellington . . . and Melba Liston, playing trombone, one of the great-
> est trombone players at that time. She could outblow most guys . . .
> So we had a remarkable band. But it's a funny thing. We rehearsed
> there in Philadelphia for about three or four weeks, really getting
> together . . . We were going to start in Billie's home, Baltimore,
> Maryland. The first day there were seven thousand people. Things
> started out really great. The next day we were in Virginia Beach,
> a good day there too, by the way. But then things began to hap-
> pen. All of the dances after that became flops. We don't know if
> it was such bad promotion or what, but in the end I remember—
> I remember this so well—here we were out on the road and we
> weren't making any money, and the money that I had saved with
> Dizzy Gillespie, Illinois Jaquet, writing in New York—we even had
> to get Melba Liston to invest some of her money in this thing."
> (Wilson 1996)

The tour with Billie Holiday soon folded. Even the tour bus company
refused to continue, as it was not receiving payment, and returned to
New York with those musicians wanting to return there. Wilson felt no
need to go back to New York and was ready to return home. He got off
the bus somewhere near Kansas City and headed to Los Angeles. Wilson
was embittered, but soon after the incident, Holiday called him to ask if
he would travel to San Diego to rehearse Charlie Barnet's band, which

*was backing her for an engagement at Tops, one of the major clubs there.
Wilson did go and rehearse the band, and he later recalled that "all of
a sudden I lost all of this terrible feeling I had about this bad luck that I
had with Billie Holiday, and I realized what a great thing that had happened to me to be able to be with Billie Holiday and to hear her singing
there. And that was the end of it. We were friends again and I didn't care
whether I got the money or not" (Wilson 1996).*

DECADE OF THE FIFTIES

*For over ten years, until 1961, Gerald Wilson would not lead a steady
orchestra, although he did assemble an array of big bands for various
recordings or performances. In his book on West Coast jazz, Ted Gioia
notes that Wilson, perhaps referring to the decade during which he was
without a regular orchestra, had commented, "Your first ten years are
thrown away . . . If you did pretty good for ten years, you're just starting"
(Watrous 1988: B6). Gioia's reading of the comment is that*

Wilson is perhaps making a virtue of necessity—as well as outlin-
ing his autobiography. The lack of recording opportunities determined that his work as a bandleader during the 1950s would be
ten years largely lost to posterity. Comebacks are, however, part of
the Wilson arsenal: Both his 1960s Pacific recordings as well as the
later 1980s releases for the Discovery label (with his "Orchestra of
the '80," as he called it), indicated that Wilson's skills did not suffer
from long layoffs. (Gioia 1992: 142–43)

*But the 1950s were not a layoff. Wilson continued his musical studies by
applying himself to a diversity of work—the very goal of his decision to
study more music, as he aimed to explore the spaces of composition, film,
television, and other creative avenues.*

*One example of this foray into other arenas was his appointment in
1950 as musical director of the* Joe Adams Show, *which ran for twenty-
five weeks on local Los Angeles television station KTTV, Channel 11. Joe
Adams was a highly popular disc jockey and hosted the program, which
was a musical variety format featuring different musical artists each*

week. Silsbee (1996: 11) notes that "Wilson was writing and arranging new
music each week but was never seen on camera. He conducted his band
off camera, but onscreen Adams was seen waving his arms in front of the
band." Ramsey writes that "through the 1950s that was typical television
policy regarding black musicians" (2000: 3).

Another Hollywood-related opportunity (briefly referred to by Wilson
in chapter 3) arose during the MGM production of the 1951 film musical
An American in Paris, *inspired by George Gershwin's music and his 1928*
symphonic tone poem. This classic, monumental film was directed by
Vincente Minnelli, produced by Arthur Freed, written by Alan Jay Lerner,
and starred Gene Kelly and Leslie Caron. It received six Academy Awards,
including those for Best Picture and Best Musical Score. Along with Benny
Carter and other Los Angeles-based jazz musicians, Wilson was featured
in a cameo role as a member of a performing jazz group in a small club.

In 1951, Wilson relocated with his wife, Josefina, to San Francisco, where
they stayed until 1954. He formed a band in the Bay Area that "included
trombonist Bob Collins, pianist Cedric Haywood, and two saxophonists,
Jerry Dodgion and Jerome Richardson, who would become mainstays of
the New York jazz scene in the late '50s and early '60s" (ibid.). Dodgion and
Richardson would also become essential members of the Thad Jones-Mel
Lewis big band based in New York.

Returning to Los Angeles in 1954, Wilson assembled another big band
at a point that he has described as the onset of his "commercial period." "I
was doing a lot of writing in those days for shows, at the Moulin Rouge in
Las Vegas and other places, and for rhythm and blues artists, Jackie Davis
among others. My deal in those days was mostly writing and orchestrating.
The big band worked whenever we had an engagement" (Ramsey 2000: 3).
Silsbee (1996: 12) adds more detail to Wilson's work during the period:

> Although he maintained a jazz orchestra, Wilson actively sought
> all kinds of work. Signing with Buck Ram, manager of the Platters,
> Wilson was kept exceptionally busy. During this ten-year period
> Wilson did such diverse things as arrange a string album for Tony
> Williams of the Platters; organize a B. B. King date for King Records
> (with Wilson, Pete Candoli and Maynard Ferguson on trumpets);
> orchestrate and play muted trumpet solos for Sam Cooke on RCA;
> guest-star, playing a jazz trumpeter, on the TV show *The Lineup*,

starring Jack Lord; handle the music for a Roy Brown date on Capitol, reprising Brown's earlier hit, "Good Rockin' Tonight"; arrange Ed Townsend's pop hit "For Your Love" on Capitol, with Eric Dolphy, René Hall and Red Callender in the studio band; and write and arrange albums for Nancy Wilson, Bobby Darin and Barbara Dane.

In 1950, the Gerald Wilson Orchestra was recorded live at Veteran's Memorial in San Francisco. However, these recordings were not released until 2006 as bonus tracks on the reissue of Wilson's 1954 Big Band Modern *LP. As noted by Matias Rinar, the tracks included are "an essential addition to Wilson's recorded legacy, and an extremely important discographic discovery" (Rinar 2006). Especially germane to these points is the fact that Wilson, with the exception of the 1954 LP cited hereafter, did not record under his own name from 1947 to 1961.*

As previously noted, Wilson's band at this point exhibited high levels of experimentation and innovation within a very bop-oriented style. His arrangements and compositions were brash, exciting, and complex. Wilson's original piece, "Hollywood Freeway," is a prime example, and two recorded versions are included on the bonus tracks. One features guest soloist Sonny Criss on a high-energy and progressive alto saxophone in addition to another "unknown" alto saxophonist, possibly Sonny Stitt or Willie Smith (see Rinar 2006). Other guest soloists included Wardell Grey, Stan Getz, and Zoot Sims, which was certainly quite a lineup.

Many younger jazz musicians of this period were consistently mentored by Wilson. One testimony is that of Horace Tapscott in his autobiographical book Songs of the Unsung:

The musicians' union was segregated then, with the black Local 767 on Central Avenue and the white Local 47 downtown. . . . Every black musician in the world would pass by there, slap you upside the head, and say something smart to you . . . Me, Eric Dolphy, Don Cherry, Frank Morgan, Hadley Caliman . . . It was just rich, very rich. . . .

Gerald was the first guy that got me into arranging and composing for a big orchestra. I met him on Central one day when I was walking home from Percy McDavid's rehearsal at Lafayette Junior

High. I had my trombone with me, and as I passed the union, Gerald walked out and said, "Hey, young blood, can you play that instrument?"

I went upstairs and there was his band, with Melba Liston playing first trombone . . . Melba said sweetly, "Sit down, young baby, sit here."

I thought, "This woman is playing trombone?"

Then she gave me the music, and it had her name on it, a tune called "Delusions." They hit the first note and that was the end of it . . . I didn't know where the hell the people were. . . . Melba knew my heart was broken, so she gave me the chart.

When I saw Gerald's writing, I had never seen anything like that in my life . . . I couldn't follow any of those charts. So I kept coming until I got it. (2001: 27–29)

It was Wilson who eventually paid for Tapscott's initial membership into the musicians' union. And Tapscott recalled another aspect of the mentorship of Wilson and others:

. . . hard drugs started coming onto Central Avenue. I got through it because of the mentors I had . . . including Gerald Wilson. . . . (2001: 47–48)

. . . in the late 1950s, when I was at the [Las Vegas] Flamingo with Gerald Wilson's band. One night Gerald said, "Tonight, we're going to break the color line." And I was ready for that. The whole band just got up from the stage and walked into the casino. (2001: 64)

THE HOLLYWOOD FILM INDUSTRY

It was during the late 1950s that Gerald Wilson began scoring for major Hollywood motion pictures. Among the more commercially and artistically successful were Anatomy of a Murder *(1959) and* Where the Boys Are *(1960).* Anatomy of a Murder, *a classic film released by Columbia Pictures and produced and directed by Otto Preminger, featured a score by Duke Ellington, including much scoring and orchestrations by Gerald*

Wilson, who also performed trumpet in the ensemble that Ellington assembled for the recording of the score. A masterpiece of cinema, the film is an intense drama of a courtroom rape trial and features actors James Stewart, Ben Gazzara, Lee Remick, George C. Scott, Arthur O'Connell, and Eve Arden. The jazz track is one of the most unique sound tracks of its period and into the present. Where the Boys Are, a satiric comedy released by MGM that also deals with rape, was written by George Wells and based on the novel by Glendon Swarthout. Actors featured included popular singer and recording artist Connie Francis and Paula Prentiss. Gerald Wilson was contracted and proceeded to score sections of the film, and was never given credit. To this day, Wikipedia (2012) notes the inclusion of compositions by Pete Rugolo and the ambience of a "West Coast" jazz musical sound track referring the styles of Dave Brubeck, Gerry Mulligan, and Chico Hamilton, popular West Coast jazz artists of the time. But Wilson remains unmentioned.

CHAPTER 5

PACIFIC JAZZ

Music's strength . . . [is] the way everything can come together
politically and spiritually, without reading books.
—NII NOI NORTEY

*In the summer of 1960, John F. Kennedy was nominated for president at
the Los Angeles Sports Arena. He took office in January of 1961. At the
age of forty-four, he was the youngest president ever elected in the United
States of America. The decade of the 1960s would be marked by youth, new
ideas, and new, complex challenges. It would be a decade like no other in
the history of the country.*

*Within this new matrix of new ideas and innovative spirit, or what
Kennedy referred to as the "New Frontier," artists would continue to create
new and innovative expressions—expressions that would keenly identify
with both the positive and negative aspects of culture, politics, and the
spirit. It would be a decade during which jazz musicians would perhaps
accelerate in style and meaning like never before, as in the likes of Miles
Davis, John Coltrane, and Ornette Coleman, or in the emerging rock
culture embodied by the diverse faces of Jimi Hendrix, Cream, and Carlos
Santana. It was a world changing at a very fast pace.*

*Gerald Wilson fit into this scenario. He was two years younger than
John Kennedy, and like Kennedy, one could say at the top of his game. He
was prepared, and he was young. But he was not the kind of young that
many artists climax at with wide acclamation and critical success. Most
importantly, he was ready to apply what he had spent years studying and
apprenticing for.*

54

THE GERALD WILSON ORCHESTRA AND PACIFIC JAZZ RECORDS, 1961–69

In 1957, Wilson initiated a workshop rehearsal band in Los Angeles to perform his compositions and arrangements. By 1961, the Gerald Wilson Orchestra debuted and was soon recording on the Pacific Jazz Records label, which would release ten of the orchestra's albums within a span of eight years. A description of this run of Wilson's work appeared in a promotional brochure published by Mosaic Records (2003) which had compiled a complete set of Wilson's Pacific Jazz recordings.

Thus began the most exciting and successful modern jazz big band to come to prominence in the early '60s. Wilson was bursting with ideas. Bebop. The blues. Modal harmonies. Mexican influences. And every idea writ large, sometimes in expansive eight-part harmony. As a leader, he allowed his musicians ample latitude for their own expressive voices, creating moods that led to music filled with feeling . . . His work for Pacific Jazz garnered instant radio play and rave reviews across the United States. And audiences noticed. (11)

The president of Pacific Jazz Records was Richard Bock, who had recorded a number of high-profile jazz artists in what came to be recognized as West Coast Jazz. Included in Bock's catalogue were records featuring the music of Gerry Mulligan, Chet Baker, Art Pepper, Jimmy Heath, Bud Shank, and Bob Gordon, among others. In an interview with Doug Ramsey (2000: 3), Wilson recalled the chain of events.

I knew Dick Bock and had followed his work. The first time I approached him about recording, in 1953, was at a Billy Eckstine record date I was visiting. And there were other occasions through the '50s when I ran into him and brought it up. He explained that, for various reasons, it was hard to record a big band. But in 1960, he called me. He had set up a deal through Albert Marx to record me.

Marx was the president of both Discovery and Trend Records. Ramsey (ibid.) notes that as they do today, Wilson's sidemen constituted a cross section of Los Angeles jazz players, black and white, youngsters and veterans, from the studios and the clubs. They had in common the musicianship Wilson could quickly observe and sometimes sense in a potential member. His leadership is based on mutual respect and his magnetism, not on strictness. He has more in common with Ellington and Herman than with disciplinarians like Benny Goodman, Tommy Dorsey and Buddy Rich.

The first recording session for Pacific Jazz occurred on September 9, 1961, at Pacific Jazz Studios in Los Angeles. Recorded that day were "Blues for Yna Yna," featuring trumpeter Carmell Jones, "The Wailer," written by Wilson for the television police series The Lineup, *and "Straight Up and Down." On September 30, the record repertoire was completed with the recording of "You Better Believe It," "Yvette" (from Wilson's film score of* Where the Boys Are*), "Jeri" (named for Wilson's eight-year-old daughter, Geraldine), and "Moody Blue." Titled* You Better Believe It, *the album was released in 1961 and featured Richard "Groove" Holmes on organ. Comprising the band were the following musicians, who vary from one recording date to the other: Ray Triscari, Jimmy Zito, John Audino, Carmell Jones, Al Porcino, Jack Trainor, trumpets; Bob Edmondson, Lester Robertson, John Ewing, Kenny Shroyer, Frank Strong, trombones; Buddy Collette, Harry Klee, Harold Land, Teddy Edwards, Jack Nimitz, Joe Maini, Walter Benton, Don Raffell, woodwinds; Richard Holmes, organ; Gene Edwards, guitar; Jimmy Bond, bass; and Mel Lewis, drums.*

Wilson's second Pacific Jazz album, Moment of Truth, *was recorded in August and September of 1962. The title track is a blues piece featuring tenor saxophonist Teddy Edwards, guitarist Joe Pass, and pianist Jack Wilson. Also on the LP was an arrangement of Miles Davis's "Milestones" and "Kind of Blue," the latter featuring, among others, Harold Land on tenor saxophone. Two of Wilson's compositions on the record were named after his daughters, "Teri" and "Nancy Jo." Also of note on the* Moment of Truth *album was the participation of drummer Mel Lewis, then based in Los Angeles but who within a few years would co-lead with Thad Jones a major jazz orchestra based in New York.*

The most impactful track on the album was Wilson's composition "Viva Tirado," which was later recorded by the Latin rock group El Chicano in 1970, emerging as a hit record, and was also adapted by rapper Kid Frost

*in 1990. Named for Mexican bullfighter José Ramón Tirado, Wilson re-
membered him as "a young matador I first saw at the bullfights in Tijuana,
Mexico. He was sensational, had a lot of style, reminds me of one of the
young trumpeters of today. I was so impressed that I wanted to give my
impression jazz-wise of what was going on with him" (Ramsey 2000: 5).*

*Other tunes on the LP included "Latino" and the beautiful, richly or-
chestrated and voiced "Josefina," dedicated to Wilson's wife and featuring
an intricate and expressive lead melody on tenor saxophone by Harold
Land. This recording also became the opening theme for Wilson's KABC
radio show* Jazz Capsule *during the 1970s, and one of Wilson's signature
stylistic pieces.* Moment of Truth *featured the following personnel among
the two recording dates: Carmell Jones, Jules Chaikin, John Audino, Freddie Hill, Al Porcino, trumpets; Bob Edmondson, Lou Blackburn, Frank
Strong, Bob Knight, Lester Robertson, trombones; Bud Shank, Joe Maini,
Teddy Edwards, Harold Land, Don Raffell, Jack Nimitz, woodwinds; Jack
Wilson, piano; Joe Pass, guitar; Jimmy Bond, bass; Mel Lewis, drums;
Modesto Duran, congas.*

In December of 1963 and January of 1964, Portraits, *Wilson's third
Pacific Jazz album was recorded. It featured soloists Carmell Jones, Teddy
Edwards, Harold Land, Jack Wilson, and Joe Pass, among others. One of
Wilson's compositions was dedicated to the North Indian sitarist Ravi
Shankar ("Ravi"), while "Aram" is a tribute to Armenian composer Aram
Khachaturian, whose music Wilson had gravitated toward during his
period of intense musical study. "Eric" was dedicated by Wilson to the
great Eric Dolphy, whom he had mentored during Dolphy's younger days
in Los Angeles and who at this time had emerged as a major jazz artist in
New York and Europe. Dolphy would tragically die of complications from
diabetes in Berlin on June 28, 1964, just months after Wilson's dedicatory
composition to him was recorded. On his first album date as a leader in
1960* (Outward Bound, *New Jazz Records), Dolphy had actually dedicated
an original piece to Wilson, titled for Wilson's initials, "G. W.," a freshly
unique composition of progressive melodic-rhythmic-harmonic form. In
the liner notes to that recording (the Prestige label's 1963 edition) Dolphy
was quoted, remarking,*

I was helped greatly by Gerald Wilson. Here is a man who has been
making the modern sounds since the war years. He had a band in
1944 that would still be considered modern today . . . [He] did a

lot for me. He would take me around to hear all the musicians and explain things to me. I owe an awful lot to this man. (Levin 1963)

On the same premier album, Dolphy also recorded an original tribute piece for Lester Robertson, who had played in Dolphy's band in Los Angeles in addition to being a trombonist in Wilson's orchestra for every one of the Pacific Jazz LPs. Dolphy was born and musically trained in Los Angeles, played with the big bands of Gerald Wilson and Roy Porter, and was a member of Chico Hamilton's group from 1958 to 1959, at which time he left Hamilton to relocate to New York, where he eventually emerged as one of the major innovative jazz musicians on the scene. In addition to many performances and recordings in New York and Europe, he performed and recorded extensively with Charles Mingus, John Coltrane, Booker Little, Ornette Coleman, Oliver Nelson, and George Russell, among many other leading artists. He is among the most acclaimed names in the history of jazz.

A few more testimonies should be included here concerning Dolphy's relationship and respect for Gerald Wilson. For example, Dolphy also stated the following:

He's very encouraging and helpful to all young musicians, no matter how well he may be doing himself. He keeps everybody aroused and interested in music. It's so important because otherwise so many people would have nothing to look forward to and no hope of being able to earn their own way in music. I have recorded an arrangement he wrote eighteen years ago—it hasn't been released yet—and it sounded so fresh. (Simosko and Tepperman 1971: 31)

In their book on Dolphy, Simosko and Tepperman wrote that "Eric definitely recorded with Gerald Wilson at some point during the mid-1950s, but no information is available. Wilson himself has stated that he has moved around so much that he can't find anything. Existing discographies fail to clarify the situation, as details on Wilson's record dates are quite hazy for that period of his career" (ibid: 31).

Lillian Polen, a close friend of Dolphy during the 1950s, made the following recollections about Dolphy's closeness to both Red Callender and Wilson:

In the little house Eric's father built for him, he was a gracious host. No matter when you fell by his pad, you were always welcome—all strangers welcome—without calling in advance; dealing with the usual social graces was not part of Eric's style of life, although he was raised that way. All were welcome. Some evenings I would come by and he would be engrossed in quiet conversation with Red Callender—but with Red and his reserve, one had to be cool. Then there would be Gerald Wilson, and the air would be filled with such fine gentleness—but that was Gerald. It appeared that Eric was to all what they wanted of him—raucous with those who were; he somehow knew that was expected of him. (Simosko and Tepperman 1971: 37)

Another interesting anecdote with reference to Dolphy's respect for Wilson was written by jazz critic Martin Williams in his foreword to the Simosko and Tepperman book:

Eric Dolphy loved jazz and he loved all music. I once heard him speak, almost in the same paragraph, of his joyful enthusiasm for the pioneer clarinetist Jimmy Noone, of his pleasure in Gerald Wilson's latest recording, and of his discovery of Karlheinz Stockhausen. It was a joy to hear him speak of music. And it was a privilege to hear him play. (ibid.: viii)

Two pieces evoking Spain on the Portraits *LP were "Paco" and "Caprichos." "Paco" was another Wilson tribute to bullfighters, this time to the Spanish matador Paco Camino. In 2000, Wilson reflected on the inspiration upon which he composed the piece:*

Paco Camino became the biggest man in the bull ring during that period. He came on with some new stuff that was out of sight. Bull fighting is not a sport, you know. It's an art, continually evolving with new passes, new uses of the cape, new ways of confronting the bull, adding to the repertoire. It's very much like jazz. Paco was an artist. He improvised. He was the best. (Ramsey 2000: 7)

"Caprichos" (translated from the Spanish as "Fantasies") featured soloists Jack Wilson, Bud Shank on flute, Joe Pass, and Harold Land. Wilson also commented on this composition:

> I was into classical music for a number of years, writing pieces with deep harmonic structure. I was into the music of Spain and particularly Manuel de Falla. He wrote *El Amor Brujo* in 1918, and it contained, harmonically, the same things that we are doing today. He could have been right here with us. Everything that Jack Wilson plays was written. There is no improvisation in his solo. (ibid.)

The personnel for the Portraits *album included the following musicians: Al Porcino, Carmell Jones, Jules Chaikin, Freddie Hill, Nat Meeks, trumpets; Bob Edmondson, John Ewing, Lester Robertson, Don Switzer, trombones; Joe Maini, Jimmy Woods, Teddy Edwards, Harold Land, Jack Nimitz, woodwinds; Jack Wilson, piano; Joe Pass, guitar; Leroy Vinnegar, Dave Dyson, bass; Chuck Carter, drums; and Modesto Duran, bongos.*

On Stage—Wilson's fourth album on Pacific Jazz—was recorded in January and March of 1965 at both Capitol Studios and Pacific Jazz Studios. Yet another Spanish-derived piece by Wilson, "Los Moros de España," marked the first participation of vibraphonist Roy Ayers with the Gerald Wilson Orchestra; Ayers is featured in the arrangement along with Harold Land. "Who Can I Turn To?"—a tune recalling Count Basie's slow dance arrangements—features Jack Wilson on Hammond B3 organ and Teddy Edwards. Land, Ayers, and Wilson, again on organ, all solo on Wilson's waltz composition, "Ricardo." "Musette" was composed by Wilson specifically for guitarist Joe Pass, and Ramsey comments that Pass "makes the most of the opportunity to exploit the beauty in its chord structure. Wilson's simple backgrounds and Pass' economy of expression emphasize that the best musicians do not require complicated changes and multiple choruses to make their point" (2000: 8). "In the Limelight" features the underappreciated artistry of Teddy Edwards and the highly talented and active trumpeter Bobby Bryant, who was at the time working extensively in Los Angeles as a jazz artist, lead trumpet player, and for Hollywood film and television studios.

Roy Ayers continued to work with the Gerald Wilson Orchestra on the On Stage *LP and is featured on "Lighthouse Blues" along with Bryant,*

Pass, and Jack Wilson. On "El Viti," Wilson actually performs the muted trumpet melody characterizing the tune, the only time he has played trumpet on a recording by his orchestra. Ramsey notes Anthony Ortega's emergence on the arrangement, writing that "the bite and pungency of Anthony Ortega's alto saxophone solo reminds us that in the mid-'60s, free jazz was having its effect on the mainstream" (ibid.). "El Viti" was also in homage to another bullfighter, Santiago Martín Sánchez.

> El Viti was a great matador, different from any other I ever saw. He never smiled, and he was tough. I tried to trace a picture of him, as it gets down into a unique part where his stuff in the ring would get wild but not overbearing. It was a place for me to use my eight-part harmony. You'll hear the brass playing it, with two different times going at once. You know, I invented eight-part harmony. (Ramsey 2000: 8–9)

It is significant to point out that the Duke Ellington Orchestra recorded Wilson's arrangement of "El Viti" in 1966 under the title of "The Matador." Other tracks on the On Stage *album included "Lately" (arranged by Lester Robertson) and Juan Tizol's classic "Perdido." Duke Ellington also recorded this same Gerald Wilson arrangement in 1960 on his* Piano in the Background *album on Columbia Records. Featured in Wilson's recording are Anthony Ortega, Teddy Edwards, and Jack Nimitz.*

Personnel for the On Stage *LP included the following: Al Porcino, Bobby Bryant, Melvin Moore, Jules Chaikin, Freddie Hill, Nat Meeks, trumpets; Bob Edmondson, John Ewing, Lester Robertson, Don Switzer, Ernie Tack, trombones; Anthony Ortega, Curtis Amy, Teddy Edwards, Bud Shank, Harold Land, Jack Nimitz, woodwinds; Roy Ayers, vibraphone; Phil Moore III, piano; Jack Wilson, piano and organ; Joe Pass, guitar; Herbie Lewis, Victor Gaskin, bass; and Chuck Carter, bass.*

In 1965, on November 30, December 2, and a third, unknown date, Wilson recorded his fifth Pacific Jazz album. Titled Feelin' Kinda Blues, *the record covered various popular hits or jazz titles of the era, including Miles Davis' "Freddie the Freeloader," the Beatles's "Yesterday" (Lennon and McCartney), Herbie Hancock's "Watermelon Man," "One On the House" by Harry James and Ernie Wilkins, Cole Porter's "I Concentrate On You," "Well Son Shuffle" (composed and arranged by trombonist Mike*

Barone, a member of Wilson's orchestra), in addition to "When I'm Feel-
ing Kinda Blue" (Wilson gave composer's credit on this tune to his wife,
Josefina, as it was inspired by his family's ideas), a rock-styled arrange-
ment later recorded by both Duke Ellington and Al Hirt. Featured soloists
on the Feelin' Kinda Blues *LP included Anthony Ortega, Bobby Bryant,*
Teddy Edwards, Victor Feldman on vibraphone, Nat Meeks on trumpet,
Phil Moore III on piano, Curtis Amy on soprano saxophone, and Den-
nis Budimir on guitar. The complete orchestra personnel comprised the
following: Melvin Moore, Al Porcino, Freddie Hill, Jules Chaikin, Nat
Meeks, Bobby Bryant, trumpets; John Ewing, Bob Edmondson, Lester
Robertson, Fred Murell, trombones; Curtis Amy, Anthony Ortega, Teddy
Edwards, Harold Land, Jack Nimitz, woodwinds; Phil Moore III, piano;
Don Randi, organ; Victor Feldman, vibraphone; Dennis Budimir, guitar;
Buddy Woodson, bass; Mel Lee, drums; and Modesto Duran, Adolpho
Valdes, Bones Howe, percussion.

Ramsey (2000: 10) notes that with Wilson's 1966 The Golden Sword
album, his sixth with Pacific Jazz, "Wilson returned to a concentration
on his love of Mexico and Mexican music. The rhythmic excitement and
massed horns of the title piece summon up the pageantry of the bull
ring." In addition to Mexico, Wilson's work on the album also evokes the
inspiration of Spain.

Wilson arranged a novel version of the Broadway stage hit and waltz
"Man of La Mancha," which featured as soloists Anthony Ortega and
Brazilian guitarist of international note Laurindo Almeida, who was also
heard on Dick Grove's arrangement of Cuban composer Ernesto Lecuona's
"The Breeze and I," a song based on Lecuona's original "Andalucía," one of
the movements of his Andalucía Suite (the well-known "Malagueña" is
another movement of the suite). The selection on The Golden Sword *that*
rose to become another of Wilson's signature pieces was "Carlos," a tone
poem dedicated to Mexican-Spanish matador Carlos Arruza. Performing
the dynamic and Spanish paso doble-*inspired melodic theme of "Carlos"*
was trumpeter Jimmy Owens. Years later, from the 1970s on, Alex Rodri-
guez, Oscar Brashear, Ron Barrows, and Bobby Rodriguez would often
perform the trumpet solo part for this piece. It should be noted that under
the title on the music score, Wilson included the following line: "Dedicated
to Carlos Arruza and Fine Trumpet Players." It is also significant to point
out that "Carlos" was recorded on June 21, 1966, only a month after Carlos

Arruza's tragic death in a car accident on a highway en route to Mexico City.

Also on the LP was Wilson's version of "Chanson du Feu Follet" from Manuel de Falla's ballet El Amor Brujo. *Ramsey (2000) notes that trumpeter Nat Meeks "takes the spotlight . . . Wilson's treatment of the piece is markedly different from that of Gil Evans for Miles Davis in the* Sketches of Spain *album. Wilson's introduction uses eight-part harmony. He gives his sax section a recurrent riff that transforms Falla's delicate theme of regret into a blues-like waltz. Meeks, Harold Land and Roy Ayers are the soloists." (10)*

The Golden Sword *also includes "Mi Corazón," composed by Wilson and featuring William (Bill) Green and Anthony Ortega on flutes and Conte Condoli on trumpet. Wilson's "Blues Latinese," intended to evoke a Latin and Asian flavor on a minor blues number, features Ortega on alto saxophone and pianist Jack Wilson. "The Feather," also a minor blues structure arranged by Mike Barone, features vibraphonist Roy Ayers and alto saxophonist Jimmy Woods. Ramsey (ibid.) comments that Wilson "worked with Barone to incorporate into the ensemble a passage that pays tribute to Sy Oliver, Wilson's predecessor in the Lunceford band." Also on the LP was "The Serpent," which, like "The Feather," was part of Wilson's suite titled* Teotihuacán *for the historic pyramids site just outside Mexico City, and symbolizing the mythic Quetzalcóatl, the feathered serpent supernatural being of the Aztec culture. "The Serpent" features Owens, Edwards, and Jack Wilson. A direct Mexican inclusion in the LP is that of "La Mentira," the classic and richly harmonic bolero composed by Mexican Alvaro Carrillo in 1965, only a year before Wilson's recorded arrangement of it. The* Golden Sword *was recorded in June, July, and August of 1966 at TTG Studios, and the three sessions included the following personnel: Al Porcino, Jules Chaikin, Freddie Hill, Mel Moore, Jimmy Owens, Nat Meeks, Conte Condoli, trumpets; Mike Barone, John Ewing, Lester Robertson, Ernie Tack, trombones; Anthony Ortega, Jimmy Woods, Harold Land, Teddy Edwards, Jack Nimitz, William (Bill) Green, woodwinds; Roy Ayers, Victor Feldman, vibraphone; Jack Wilson, piano; Laurindo Almeida, guitar; Buddy Woodson, bass; Mel Lee, drums; and Max Garduno, congas.*

On March 31 and April 1 of 1967, the LP Live and Swinging *was recorded live during two performances by the Gerald Wilson Orchestra at*

Marty's On the Hill, a Los Angeles nightclub. One of the major changes in the orchestra was the addition of trumpeter Charles Tolliver, who had previously been working and recording with Jackie McLean, among other major jazz artists in New York, and who would later record with Max Roach, Horace Silver, and McCoy Tyner, in addition to many albums as a leader. Tolliver's own composition, "Paper Man," which would be the title track of the trumpeter's first album as a leader in 1968, is the first track on the Live and Swinging *album. Ramsey (2000) writes that*

> the piece, arrangement and Tolliver's solo are packed with nervous energy. Hadley Caliman, debuting with Wilson, is the tenor soloist. At 35 a seasoned player, Caliman was a professional at 16 and in Roy Porter's big band when he was 17. Phil Moore has replaced Jack Wilson on piano, freeing Wilson to concentrate on the organ. (12)

The album *also features Dick Grove's arrangement of "I Should Care," and Harold Land is featured on the Ellington/Webster classic "I Got It Bad (and That Ain't Good)," in addition to his own modern piece, "The IT's Where It's At," named after the famous Los Angeles jazz club. The LP also includes "New Thing," a progressive composition reflecting the contemporary movement of free and evolving jazz styles that features Land, Tolliver, and Moore, and "Blues for a Scorpio," a Mike Barone orchestration based on a theme composed by Wilson's fourteen-year-old daughter Geraldine (Jeri). Jack Wilson is featured on organ on both Neal Hefti's classic "Li'l Darlin'," originally recorded by the Count Basie Orchestra in 1957, and the Erroll Garner 1954 standard "Misty." Finally, "Viva Tirado," originally recorded on the 1962* Moment of Truth *album, is included as part of the* Live and Swinging *LP, with solos by Tolliver, Caliman, and Moore. Personnel for the live, recorded performance included Gary Barone, Dick Forrest, Larry McGuire, Alex Rodriguez, Charles Tolliver, Al Porcino, trumpets; Lester Robinson, Mike Barone, Thurman Green, Don Switzer, trombones; Ramon Bojorquez, Anthony Ortega, Harold Land, Hadley Caliman, woodwinds; Howard Johnson, baritone sax and tuba; Phil Moore III, piano; Jack Wilson, organ; Buddy Woodson, bass; and Carl Lott, drums.*

Wilson's eighth album on Pacific Jazz was Everywhere. *Ramsey (2000) makes the following notes on Wilson's title track for the album:*

It is unrelated to the piece of the same name written and performed by trombonist Bill Harris in Woody Herman's "First Herd." Wilson's "Everywhere" is an exploration of the blues in a contemporary format, with an insistent theme. He describes it as "a very classical number." He first scored it for alto saxophonist Cannonball Adderley for a concert with Stan Kenton's Neophonic Orchestra. The muscular tenor sax solo in this version is Caliman's. Jack Wilson follows on harpsichord, a predecessor of the piano forte that plucks the strings, rather than hammers them. It is a plucky solo. (12)

In keeping with Ramsey's eloquence in the latter excerpt, it seems appropriate to also refer to his picture of Wilson's arrangement of a Harold Arlen song:

Gerald's treatment of Harold Arlen's "Out of this World" has touches of Latin America and of Stravinsky. It is one of his most complex arrangements, first performed by Wilson at a 1945 concert with singer Joe Williams, a decade before Williams became famous with Count Basie. This time around Bobby Bryant gets the melody and, at the conclusion, an opportunity to strut his high-note stuff. Anthony Ortega appears on alto. Vibraphonist Bobby Hutcherson bows in with the band on "Out of this World." (ibid.)

Hutcherson, also featured on Michel LeGrand's "Pretty Polly," had already emerged as one of the premier jazz vibraphonists in the country. Originally from Los Angeles, he had already recorded with Jackie McLean, Eric Dolphy, and Dexter Gordon, and would go on to record extensively with both his own groups and in collaborations with Harold Land (with whom he co-led a group that recorded four albums), Lee Morgan, Freddie Hubbard, Woody Shaw, Joe Henderson, Herbie Hancock, and McCoy Tyner, among many other leading jazz artists and recording projects.

The piece "M. Capetillo," to quote Ramsey again, "joins the honorees in Wilson's gallery of bullfighting heroes" (ibid.). Wilson had been present at a Tijuana bull ring for Manuel Capetillo's last bullfight, and the composition features Harold Land and Joe Pass, who returned to the band after some years of not recording with Wilson, as his own career as a solo artist had achieved a high level of success. Other tracks on the album include "Little Bit of Soul," a funk blues featuring Ortega on piccolo, Richard Aplanalp on baritone saxophone, and Caliman on tenor saxophone. Hutcherson and Land are featured on Wilson's arrangement of the Rodgers and Hammerstein's "Do I Love You (Because You're Beautiful?)" from the stage musical Cinderella.

The LP includes another musical portrait of a bullfighter by Wilson, this time that of Antonio Del Olivar. Like many of his other matador models, Wilson had known Del Olivar, who once honored Wilson with the traditional presentation of the bull's ear after the close of a bullfight. Along with Paco Camino, the model for one of Wilson's previous dedications to matadors, Del Olivar was one of the dominant bullfighters during the sixties and seventies. Ramsey refers to this piece, titled "Del Olivar," as "a tone poem with classical leanings . . . Once again, Wilson combines two of his favorite idioms, the waltz and the blues" (13). The album Everywhere closes out with Wilson's "Mini Waltz," highlighted by an elegant and precise performance by Bobby Hutcherson in addition to a richly crafted alto saxophone solo by Ramon Bojorquez. Personnel on the LP, recorded on December 4, 1967 and January 2, 1968, at Liberty Studios, consisted of the following musicians: Dick Forrest, Steve Huffsteter, Alex Rodriguez, Bill Mattison, Bobby Bryant, Gary Barone, trumpets; Frank Strong, Lester Robertson, Thurman Green, Mike Wimberly, trombones; Anthony Ortega, Ramon Bojorquez, Harold Land, Hadley Caliman, Richard Aplanalp, William (Bill) Green, Henry De Vega, woodwinds; Bobby Hutcherson, vibraphone; Jack Wilson, piano and organ, Phil Moore III, piano; Joe Pass, guitar; Buddy Woodson, Stan Gilbert, bass; Carl Lott, Frank Butler, drums; Hugh Anderson, percussion; and Moisés Obligación, congas.

By 1968, Pacific Jazz Records started branding itself as World Pacific Records, so Wilson's ninth album with the company was released on the new label. Titled California Soul, this LP consisted of arrangements of various popular songs and tunes of the period. Ramsey (13) makes some interesting comments regarding the paradox confronting jazz musicians of the era—for many, the paradox became a career crisis:

As the '60s wound down, popular music had come to have virtually nothing to do with jazz or jazz values. Jazz artists scrambled to keep a little piece of the commercial market. The logical way seemed to be to appropriate and adapt popular songs. Gerry Mulligan titled one of his albums *If You Can't Beat 'Em, Join 'Em.* That approach had worked throughout the recorded history of jazz, but for much of the music's first three or four decades the best pop songs and jazz shared artistic standards. In the swing era, astonishing as it seems now, jazz *was* popular music. After 1955, except for blues-based rock and roll hits, there was little in the Top 40 that could serve as material for improvisation or as serious subject matter for arrangers.

Wilson's penultimate Pacific Jazz album was among the most musically respectable attempts to use contemporary hits to attract audiences whose tastes had been formed by rock and roll and soul music. "Soul sound is not new," Wilson told Herb Wong in the liner notes for *California Soul.* "It all came from things that happened long ago. First it was R & B, now there are extensions with contributions from other cultures. Admittedly we are trying to reach more people — people who may not have caught our sound before." Looking back, Gerald recalls another reason. "My kids were very young," Gerald says, "and I was hearing a lot of this music around the house, on their radio and their records. So I thought I'd give a couple of those numbers a try, things by Cream, The Doors, those groups. When we'd play them at dances, people seemed to like them."

"California Soul," the album's title track, was a hit record by the popular singing quintet the Fifth Dimension. Wilson arranged the piece in a Latin vein with dynamic solos by Harold Land and Bobby Hutcherson. The Doors's "Light My Fire" is included on the record, and Wilson's arrangement is a dynamic and impressive setting of the psychedelic rock tune, highlighted by the use of piccolo (featuring Anthony Ortega's improvisations) and flute with intersecting horn sections resolving on some of Wilson's extended harmonic structures. Bobby Bryant takes a powerful and soulful solo on trumpet, and tenor saxophonist Hadley Caliman embellishes the arrangement nicely. Hutcherson is again featured on Wilson's "Channel Island," named after the islands off the southern California coast. Other tracks include "Lullaby from Rosemary's Baby," from the 1968 Hollywood film, Cream's "Sunshine of Your Love," Wilson's "Russian

River" (named after the river in northern California), and Smokey Rob-
inson's "Yesterlove," featuring tenor saxophonist Henry De Vega using the
Varitone, a multi-octave electronic effects accessory. The LP is rounded
out with Wilson's rich and soothing orchestration of Lalo Schifrin's "Down
Here On the Ground," featuring soloist Harold Land, and the Latinesque
"El Presidente."

It is possible to look back on this period of Wilson's career as one of
commercial compromise. But I do not look at it like that. Wilson accepted
the changes occurring in music and society as a reality, so his intuition told
him to not only be tolerant but creative with it. As he expressed to Herb
Wong, his kids were involved in these expressive forms and new styles.
He was also challenging the race chasm by interpreting the fields of both
hard rock and contemporary soul. Wilson has continually looked on the
bright side.

He was also trying to keep working, and to keep his musicians working.

Recorded in three sessions in August and September of 1968, personnel
on California Soul was made up of the following musicians: Larry Mc-
Guire, Alex Rodriguez, Tony Rusch, Ollie Mitchell, Dalton Smith, trumpets; Frank Strong, Lester Robertson, Thurman Green, Mike Wimberly,
trombones; Art Maebe, French horn, tuba; Jim McGee, George Hyde,
French horns; Anthony Ortega, Ramon Bojorquez, Hadley Caliman, Harold Land, Richard Aplanalp, Henry De Vega, William Green, Pete Terry,
Alan Beutler, Bill Perkins, woodwinds; Bobby Hutcherson, vibraphone;
Tommy Flanagan, Jimmy Rowles, Mike Wofford, piano, organ, electric
harpsichord; Mike Anthony, guitar; Wilton Felder, electric bass; Stan Gilbert, bass; Carl Lott, drums; and Hugh Anderson, Joe Porcaro, percussion.

On his tenth and final album on the Pacific Jazz/World Pacific Jazz labels, Eternal Equinox, Wilson abandons the hit cover concept of the previous
LP and returns to his more natural home of compositions in the jazz idiom
(with the exception of the Ashford and Simpson hit "Aquarius" from the hit
musical Hair and Smokey Robinson's "Baby, Baby Don't Cry"). Also returning is organist Richard "Groove" Holmes, who had recorded on Wilson's
premier Pacific Jazz LP You Better Believe It of 1961. Holmes and Harold
Land are featured on Wilson's beautiful and resounding rendering of John
Coltrane's "Equinox." This track of Wilson's arrangement is one of the most
frequent jazz radio playlist inclusions to the present day. It is a classic.

In many ways, Eternal Equinox *serves as a musical and social metaphor for Wilson's way of expression and survival through the decade beginning in 1960 and ending in 1969, the release year of this LP. From the election of John Kennedy to his assassination, in addition to those of Dr. Martin Luther King, Malcolm X, and Robert Kennedy, to race riots from Watts to Detroit and the passing of the Civil Rights Act, the period was one that can be assessed through the music of Gerald Wilson. As Samuel A. Floyd Jr. notes, "with the emergence of this quest for black power, African Americans donned new masks—dashikis and Afros—Signifyin(g) turned inward and sometimes ugly, and one of the musics of black protest was a new and angry jazz" (1995: 184). Floyd cites Miles Davis and John Coltrane as the leading jazz figures of the 1960s, and senses that*

the apparently contradictory stances and actions of the period manifested themselves multifariously, with the philosophies of King and Malcolm X representing contrasting views of the struggle for freedom. These two perspectives, and the activities each spawned, expressed the prevailing philosophical struggles of the black community in a period characterized by an unusual juxtaposition of pessimism and optimism, idealism and pragmatism in a social, political, and cultural cauldron from which would spring, ironically, a new intellectual and artistic energy, a new cultural awakening. (184)

"Pisces" is another beautiful composition on Eternal Equinox, *exhibiting counterpunching horn sections exploiting an impressive range of dynamics and precise execution. Ramsey (14) notes that "Coltrane's spirit" seems to guide Wilson's piece, which he describes as "a polished example, particularly in the opening and closing ensembles, of Wilson's ways of setting reeds and brass off against one another. Ortega's fiery solo is deep into the freedom that developed in jazz following the emergence of Ornette Coleman and the modal and scalar improvisational approaches put forward by Miles Davis, Bill Evans and Coltrane in Davis'* Kind of Blue *period." Of note on the arrangement is the virtuoso work and improvisation of Bobby Hutcherson, who offers rich and impeccably crafted concepts and progressive development on the vibraphone.*

Wilson's "Scorpio Rising" is equally impressive, another progressive composition and arrangement with virtuoso jazz improvisation, this time by the French guest violinist Jean-Luc Ponty, which Ramsey (15) refers to as "one of his best recorded violin solos of the decade." Ponty had emerged as a major artist in jazz, fusion, and rock, and became a member of guitarist John McLaughlin's Mahavishnu Orchestra. Wilson's "Celestial Soul" features the orchestra's newly added tenor saxophonist, Ernie Watts, who previously played with Buddy Rich's big band and who would become a regular member of Doc Severinsen's band featured on the NBC television network Tonight Show *with Johnny Carson. Watts's solo on the piece is intricately tasty, and Holmes's organ provides funky yet smooth interpretations. On Wilson's arrangement of Smokey Robinson's "Baby, Baby Don't Cry," actor William Marshall recites the song's lyrics in a stately, resonant, soulful style, followed by Harold Land's improvisations. George Duke's progressive and high-energy, virtuosic piano highlights Wilson's other pieces on the LP, "You, Me and Now" and the well-orchestrated "Bluesnee," which also features tenor saxophonist Hadley Caliman. Pianist Duke at this time was emerging as a major innovator in jazz, fusion, and rock contexts. Ramsey (15) makes another insightful remark, noting that "Wilson's writing is absolutely up to date, or a bit beyond, while observing the eternal blues truths."*

The LP Eternal Equinox *was recorded on three dates in June of 1969, and the personnel included the following: Larry McGuire, Jay Daversa, Paul Hubinon, Tony Rusch, William Peterson, trumpets; Lester Robinson, Frank Strong, Thurman Green, Alexander Thomas, Mike Wimberly, trombones; Arthur Maebe, French horn; Henry De Vega, Anthony Ortega, William Green, Ernie Watts, Hadley Caliman, Harold Land, Richard Aplanalp, Bud Shank, woodwinds; Jean-Luc Ponty, violin; William Marshall, cello; Bobby Hutcherson, vibraphone; Richard Holmes, organ; George Duke, piano; Wilbert Longmire, guitar; Bob West, electric and acoustic bass; and Carl Lott, Paul Humphrey, drums.*

BEYOND PACIFIC JAZZ: WORK WITH THE GREAT JAZZ VOCALISTS

Previously covered in various sections of this book is the musical association of Wilson with such historic vocalists of jazz, including Billy Eckstine,

Herb Jeffries, Dinah Washington, Joe Williams, and Billie Holiday. Others included Al Hibbler, Johnny Hartman, Bobby Darin, and Carmen Mc-Crae. During the 1960s, Wilson would work closely with four of the most prominent singers in jazz history: Ella Fitzgerald, Sarah Vaughan, Nancy Wilson, and Ray Charles.

Released in 1962 on the ABC Paramount label and recorded in New York City and Los Angeles was the Ray Charles album Modern Sounds in Country and Western Music. *By this time, Charles had emerged as a leading rhythm and blues artist, but his musical style was as rooted in jazz as it was in gospel, blues, and soul. Wilson did four of the arrangements on the LP and Gill Fuller did two; the remaining six were string and choral backdrops by Marty Paich. One of the tracks, "I Can't Stop Loving You," also released as a single, garnered a 1962 Grammy Award for Best R & B Recording/Best Rhythm and Blues Performance. In his review of the album, Stephen Cook comments that the LP*

fit right in with Ray Charles' expansive musical ways while on the Atlantic label in the '50s. In need of even more room to explore, Charles signed with ABC Paramount and eventually took full advantage of his contract's "full artistic freedom clause" with this collection of revamped country classics. Covering a period from 1939 to the early '60s, the 12 tracks here touch on old-timey fare (Floyd Tillman's "It Makes No Difference to Me Now"), honky tonk (three Hank Williams songs), and early countrypolitan (Don Gibson's "I Can't Stop Loving You"). Along with a Top Ten go at Eddy Arnold's "You Don't Know Me," the Gibson cover helped the album remain at the top of the pop charts for nearly three months and brought Charles international fame. Above a mix of swinging big band charts by Gerald Wilson and strings and choir backdrops from Marty Paich, Charles intones the sleepy-blue nuances of country crooners while still giving the songs a needed kick with his gospel outbursts. No pedal steel or fiddles here, just a fine store of inimitable interpretations. (Cook 2013)

In their text on American popular music, Starr and Waterman (2010) note that Modern Sounds in Country and Western Music *"stands as a milestone in the history of American popular music. . . . By this point,*

Charles was aggressively and creatively playing with stylistic mixtures, and the album essentially redrew the map of American popular music, both appealing to and challenging fans of radically different genres" (281). Ray Charles followed up with a second volume of the Country and West-ern *LP title, which he recorded in both New York City and Hollywood with his own big band. As in Volume I, he used his backup singers, the Raelettes, in addition to strings and chorus. More hits ensued, notably "You Are My Sunshine," arranged by Gerald Wilson.*

Nineteen sixty-three was an especially busy year in regards to his work with jazz vocalists, as Wilson arranged and conducted on albums released that year by both Sarah Vaughan and Nancy Wilson. On Vaughn's Sarah Sings Soulfully *LP on the Roulette Birdland label, twelve tracks feature Wilson's arranging of both jazz standards and contemporary popular hits of the day. In his notes to the album, Teddy Reig described the record as "another collection of [Vaughn's] total artistry . . . Backed by arrangements from the pen of Gerald Wilson, she renders with stunning effect, soulful meaning . . . At the hands of Sarah Vaughan and Gerald Wilson, these songs achieve an even brighter sparkle—one that lights up every moment of this recording" (1963). Among the tracks were "A Taste of Honey," "What Kind of Fool Am I?" "Moanin'," and "Round Midnight."*

Nancy Wilson's Yesterday's Love Songs . . . Today's Blues *featured Wilson's arrangements along with his orchestra on the album's twelve tracks, including "The Song Is You," "Satin Doll," "Bewitched," "Suffering With the Blues," "Someone to Watch over Me," "The Best Is Yet to Come," "All My Tomorrows," and "Blue Prelude," among others. Barbara Gardner, who wrote the liner notes, referred to the LP as Nancy Wilson's "finest effort to date," proceeding to comment on her association with Wilson's arranging and orchestra:*

It is a high tribute to her musicianship that Miss Wilson has been recorded with an impressive list of prominent jazz musicians. Her outing here with the blossoming Gerald Wilson big band is a wor-thy continuation of this tradition.

Gerald Wilson has provided a perfect setting for the singer, and his advanced big band charts skillfully and meaningfully aug-ment every nuance Miss Wilson attempts. That strings need not be saccharine or mushy is capably illustrated here in the execution of the four ballads set against a strings background. (Gardner 1963)

In 1969, Wilson served as arranger and conductor on Ella Fitzgerald's final album for Reprise Records. Released in 1970 and produced by Norman Granz, Things Ain't What They Used to Be *(And You Better Believe It) consisted of newer popular repertoire such as "Sunny," a hit song written and recorded by Bobby Hebb, a cover of Sergio Mendes's Brazil 66's recording of Jorge Ben's "Mas Que Nada," "Days of Wine and Roses" (Mancini/ Mercer), and Marvin Gaye's "Heard It Through the Grapevine." Jazz standards included the classic Cubop "Manteca" (Gillespie/Pozo/Fuller) and the title track, Mercer Ellington's "Things Ain't What They Used to Be."*

In addition to many of Wilson's regular orchestra musicians, the recording also included some of the other leading jazz artists of the time, including pianists Tommy Flanagan and Joe Sample, drummer Louis Bellson, and trumpeter Harry "Sweets" Edison. The arrangements on the LP were complex, progressive, and rhythmically exciting, emphasizing a good amount of Latin percussion, as well as improvised stylizing and scatting by Ella Fitzgerald.

CHAPTER 6

FROM THE SEVENTIES ON
Diversity and Expanding Roles

I'll tell you, if a guy came along playing a Coke bottle,
I'd wait until I heard him before I laughed.
—BOBBY BRADFORD

From the early 1970s to the days I write these notes in 2013, Wilson's musical culture and impact have, in a single word, diversified. During this time, his role has expanded well beyond that of bandleader, arranger, and composer, as he entered the realms of symphonic composition, radio, and education while all the time maintaining his principal vocation of composing, arranging, recording, concertizing, and keeping his orchestra together.

THE SYMPHONIC EXPERIENCE

During the very early years of the 1970s decade, Wilson was offered an opportunity for a commission to compose a piece for the Los Angeles Philharmonic, at that time and since 1962 directed by Zubin Mehta, who would continue to conduct the orchestra until 1978, when he was hired as conductor for the New York Philharmonic, a post he held until 1991. In his Suite Memories *(Wilson 1996), Wilson recalled the sequence of events:*

I received a call from Ray Brown, the great bassist. And he said, "Gerald, they're getting ready to do a big concert down at the

Music Center. I'm the coordinator. I would like for you to be on it. What we're going to do, the Los Angeles Philharmonic and Zubin Mehta, they're going to honor great black composers. I want you to be one of them." So I told him, "Yes, I'd be glad to." I always said I wanted to score for the symphony. That's why I had studied so very hard. You know, this is a big orchestra, a hundred and five pieces. You're talking about big bands. This is the big band. The concert went down without a hitch. The band did it great although we didn't do any jazz in it. You can hear, "This is Gerald Wilson's . . ." The number was supposed to be in honor of guess who? Malcolm X. In fact, on my score that's what it says. To this day that's what it says. *Malcom X.* They got a lot of flack a little later, and this came from a black lawyer here in Los Angeles who resented the fact that they were going to honor Malcolm X. He raised so much flack about it. There was a big article in the *Times* about it. For the concert there we changed the name of the number. The date of the concert was May 21, 1972. The title of the number is "Debut 5/21/72." Also at this time it's almost like an audition because right after that I'm hired by the Los Angeles Philharmonic to orchestrate four other numbers for the Philharmonic and a two-hundred voice choir. Zubin and I have to go down on Vermont Street to a gospel church. We spend the whole day there. We taped them singing their numbers. I just take the tape and go home and fit the orchestra around what they're singing. Incidentally, they took the music to television. The Israel Philharmonic has played this music. And I did other numbers for the Philharmonic. I did, in all, including the other people, about eight numbers in all. One, we won the prize . . . they had a big contest at the Forum here in Los Angeles. And Zubin Mehta and the choir won. They won it all. All the gospel choirs from all over the world. Besides winning the gospel competition at the Forum with Joe Esmole and his choir and everything. These were his original numbers too, by the way. I'm just the orchestrator and arranger here. I didn't compose these numbers for the choir. But we won first place on that competition and on the bicentennial. I had a number on the bicentennial at the Hollywood Bowl with Zubin Mehta and the Philharmonic. Zubin Mehta's quite a man. To my mind, this is one of the greatest conductors in the world. And of course he does play the bass. You know, that's his instrument, by the way. Of course, he's Indian. He believes in you when he knows you can do the work. That's the way he treats me. We became good friends. In fact so much so, I even wrote a jazz number for Zubin and recorded it. It's called "Blues for Zubin" and it's on one of my albums for Discovery Records. That was one of the really big highlights of my career.

SOCIAL VERSATILITY: EDUCATION AND MEDIA

During the 1970s, Wilson began to teach courses on the history of jazz at a number of different universities in the Los Angeles area. These included the University of Utah in the late 1960s, California State University, Northridge, from 1969 to 1983, California State University, Los Angeles (Cal State LA), from 1980 to 1991, California Institute of the Arts (CalArts), and the University of California, Los Angeles (UCLA), from 1992 to 2008, where his classes exceeded five hundred students in number. At UCLA, as part of the Jazz Studies program initiated by Kenny Burrell in 1996, Wilson directed, with Garnett Brown, the UCLA Jazz Orchestra till 2004. This student ensemble recorded a CD under Wilson's and Brown's direction. Through the years, Wilson has also conducted many workshops and lectures at universities, colleges, and high schools. During our interviews, I asked Wilson about this aspect of his changing career.

Loza: The last time we talked, Gerald, we were also talking about why you got so involved in education, radio, all these other areas. And then also we were just talking today about the number of appearances you've done not only with your band all over the world, but how you, for example, have worked with so many student orchestras. During the last twenty years or so, where are the places that you've gone to do this kind of work throughout the United States and other parts of the world? You just mentioned that you went to France two weeks ago. We took you to Mexico just this past fall. How many of those things have you done since you got into education by teaching the history of jazz and by also becoming a radio disc jockey with your own jazz show?

Wilson: Well, you know, at the time that I got into radio, you remember, I was trying to build my name and this was a chance to build my name. I was going to be on the radio every day with a two-hour show, you know? So it was a good chance to build my name there. As far as schools are concerned, as I said, I spent thirteen years at Northridge. I spent ten years at Cal State LA. I spent three years at CalArts out in Valencia. And I spent over fifteen years at UCLA. I've been to many universities. I can name a few to you now. I've been to, say, the University of Massachusetts in Amherst. Worked with the band there (two bands they had). And, by the way . . . the two bands . . . and that was in 1991 or something, they didn't have one black in either band. And yet at the time that I went through there and did my couple of days with them (however many days it was), Max Roach was one of the teachers there at the time. They had black teachers that were teaching there. Then I went on to the New England Conservatory. The New England Conservatory had one black in the band. He's a trombone player that's still playing. In fact, at the moment now he's going to be playing at the San Francisco Jazz Festival coming up with Joshua Redmond. He was a trombone player, excellent trombone player. They only had one. Well, they had George Russell there who was teaching . . . the Berklee School of Music, I went over and talked to them. I did a rehearsal with their band and everything. In their band I think they had one at the time. They had one black in the band! This is in the Berklee School. Just one black! Long Island U. I went to Long Island U. They had three or four blacks in their band, which was good to see. I was glad to see that. Then I went to Rutgers for a week. And that was the place that really impressed me as far as giving blacks a chance because they had about six or seven blacks in the band. Brown University in Providence, they had I think one in the band. And I found this all over the country, everywhere I went. All of the colleges out here, there were no blacks in the band, hardly. You know? And I find that to be, I think it's a "Why didn't they have any? Why didn't they have any?" And I kept wondering why didn't they have any? So it seems to me that [there might have been] a plan behind it working, because I don't think we're going to see many blacks in bands in colleges any more.

We also did the Oslo project. We've been to Italy. We've been to North Sea, played the North Sea. Played it two times. I played in London. I played in Verona. I played in Holland and, of course, Norway. And all the things I did with my band.

Loza: You have also worked with student orchestras in other countries, so compare those experiences. What was the reaction of people, students, playing your music? I'm thinking especially of Mexico, where they'd never even heard your stuff. Compare that to what you do here. How was it?

Wilson: Well, if you remember, we were there rehearsing the guys. Talking with them. And we played the concert and they came off very good. Yeah, they did very well.

Loza: You were over in Paris two weeks ago.

Wilson: The same thing. Excellent musicians. These people, we have to remember now, these people studied there for six years. Same thing in Harlem, too, by the way, at the conservatory. And I have pictures with the musicians there in Harlem. And they were good. They were very good. It's another thing when these guys go to school and they study for these years and they have to study six years to graduate. They were really good. The same thing in Norway. The musicians were very good. Now, these were professional musicians in Norway. They were not in school. They were professional musicians playing in the symphony orchestras. And playing different jazz bands that they had around the area.

Wilson's comments in the interview excerpts above represent only a fraction of the many and diverse touring and teaching projects he has experienced through the years. I was witness to three particular projects of which I can offer here direct testimony. In the late 1990s, I organized a UCLA exchange in conjunction with the Centro Nacional de Investigación, Documentación e Información Musical Carlos Chávez (CENIDIM) of the Mexican government's division of fine arts. We sent Wilson and his wife, Josefina, to Mexico City to conduct lectures, workshops, and a concert at the Centro Nacional de las Artes. Wilson lectured on the jazz tradition and concepts in addition to rehearsing and presenting a concert with the student jazz orchestra of the jazz studies program at the Escuela Superior de Música, a college-level, conservatory-type of institution. We also sent three other UCLA instructors to assist Wilson with the teaching and workshops: pianist Dwight Dickerson; drummer Sherman Ferguson; and bassist Roberto Miranda.

In 2002, I was teaching at the University of New Mexico and directing its Arts of the Americas Institute. I was also directing for one semester the student jazz orchestra there. We invited Wilson to conduct a series of lectures, workshops, and rehearsals with the ensemble, which then performed two consecutive concert dates at the Outpost jazz performance space in Albuquerque. As in Mexico City, and as always, Wilson and his dynamic knowledge and style was a complete hit.

Finally, I can attest to something that was very special. In 2005, I was given the opportunity to co-teach with Wilson his History of Jazz class for one quarter at UCLA. The idea was to help him with some of the administrative aspects of the class, as he was having some difficulty with his eyesight at the time. What I witnessed was a master teacher who was absolutely loved by his students. He taught the class, and I just watched. What makes Wilson so special is that he loved the students back, and wanted them to learn the beauty of jazz art and its inseparable relationship to the nation. And he taught what he had lived, firsthand. And not too many professors have lived the music like he has.

In 2006, Wilson was awarded the UCLA Distinguished Teaching Award for Non-Academic Senate Faculty, a recognition and honor bestowed on only a select few at UCLA.

RADIO AND JAZZ CAPSULE

In 1969, Wilson began what was to become a highly influential and popular radio program on the all-jazz station KBCA in Los Angeles.

Wilson: I was called one day by Saul Levine, the owner. At this time, they were on Wilshire Boulevard near La Brea in just a one, little-room place. I received this call from Saul Levine asking me if I'd like to do a show on his jazz station. And, of course, I'll try anything once, you know. So I told him, "Yes." I stayed there for about a year doing just on Sunday afternoons, then the station kept getting bigger and bigger and they moved out to Westwood in the McCulloch Old building which [was] on Westwood and Wilshire. So we went out there and Saul asked me if I would like to do a show five days a week, two hours a day, and I would do live interviews with musicians . . . Yes, I named my show. It was called *Jazz Capsule*. It had all of the people there. Duke Ellington. Count Basie. Sarah Vaughan. Carmen McRae. Chick Corea, even. Even the young musicians wanted . . . everybody wanted to be on this show. I had my partner there. He was a fella that had had a show. He had a few hours himself. His name was Dennis Smith, and Dennis did all of the stuff with handling the apparatus for broadcasting. All I did was talk to the people. I enjoyed that because like I said, I knew many of them and I could talk with them about what they wanted to talk about.

The radio program continued with great success until its final year in 1976. It is because of the musical, creative, and diverse spirit of Wilson, in addition to his intense involvement in education and the media, that by the 1970s he was considered to be an "institution" of jazz culture and knowledge, of the city of Los Angeles, and of the larger forces of humanity searching for answers to the divisions in society. Wilson's openness and honesty attracted both artists and non-artists of every ethnic and social persuasion. He simply epitomized diversity in every shape, color, and meaning.

THE GERALD WILSON ORCHESTRA OF THE EIGHTIES

By 1980, Wilson began marketing his band as the "Gerald Wilson Orchestra of the 80s." Although he was still employing some of his earlier stalwart members, such as Harold Land, Snooky Young, Gerald Wiggins, Bobby Bryant, Jack Nimitz, and Anthony Ortega, he was now also featuring a newer crop of younger jazz musicians, among them Ernie Watts, Oscar Brashear, Thurman Green, Garnett Brown, Milcho Leviev, and Harold Land, Jr.

In 1981, the album Lomelin *was recorded and released on the Discovery/Trend label, produced by Albert Marx, who had financed Wilson's records on Pacific Jazz that were produced by Richard Bock. The title track, "Lomelin," was another of Wilson's homages to bullfighters. Antonio Lomelin was another of the great matadors from Mexico, and especially popular among Americans from the United States who frequented the Plaza Monumental bullring in Tijuana, where Wilson witnessed so many of the* corridas. *In the composition and arrangement, Wilson again blends the Spanish/Mexican-styled* paso doble *tonal setting, with the subtle colors and harmonic innuendos of a jazz freedom. The main theme throughout the piece features, and is built around, Oscar Brashear's powerfully searing and precise trumpet, in addition to what Leonard Feather described in the liner notes as "flute commentaries by Jerome Richardson and Buddy Collette, the always virile tenor of Harold Land, Sr. and the fleet piano of Mike Wofford" (1981).*

"Ay-ee-en" is named for Wilson's son, Anthony, and his two grandsons, Eric and Nicholas. Featured on piccolo is Jerome Richardson, with both Buddy Collette and Hank DeVega on flute. Solos are improvised by Wofford, Richardson on soprano saxophone, Brashear, Bob Conti on guitar, and Harold Land Jr. on piano. "See You Later" is a blues-styled piece featuring guitarist Shuggie Otis, son of the highly successful rhythm and blues bandleader Johnny Otis, in addition to being Wilson's son-in-law. Shuggie Otis was also well known as a member of his father's band. Feather noted that the piece was "metrically unconventional, since there is a 3/4 bar that appears as the second of each four-measure stanza, while the others are in 4/4 (ibid.). The musical structure of the track "You Know," dedicated by Wilson to his producer Albert Marx, is described by Feather and Wilson as follows:

"You Know" is unusual in a couple of aspects. It starts out with a theme based on minor 11th chords, using the 11th in the bass as the root. After a modulation, the basic chord is used. "It's the kind of thing that could have gone in many directions," says Gerald, "and I wrote it with this feeling of not being constricted harmonically or melodically in any way." (Feather 1981)

"Triple Chase" is one of the LP's tracks that was still being played by the Gerald Wilson Orchestra into the second decade of the twenty-first century. It is a bop, progressive-styled showpiece for three tenor saxophone soloists, and the recording featured Ernie Watts, Harold Land Sr., and Jerome Richardson. The final solo is on guitar by Bill Conti. "Blues for Zubin" was described by Wilson as a theme that "was a piece in my first symphonic work for the Philharmonic, the one entitled '5/21/72' [previously referenced in this chapter] . . . It's just a little phrase that I thought I

could extend into a whole number" (ibid.). The arrangement features Bill Conti, Ernie Watts, and Jerome Richardson, again on piccolo.

Of significance to the Lomelin *album are the final, eloquent words written by Feather in his liner notes:*

> Little has been said here concerning the individuality of Gerald Wilson, the pervasive sense of drama, the creative force that surges through his every chart. Such comments are unnecessary, for anyone who has studied his work is well aware of these characteristics. If you are among the younger members of the Wilson cognoscenti, it would be as well for you to learn simply by listening. There is nothing in the art of describing orchestral sounds that can come close, let alone level, to the excitement of hearing the music itself. (ibid.)

Another Discovery Trend LP was released in 1983, titled Jessica *for another of Wilson's grandchildren. In addition to Wilson's two original pieces, the title track and "Blues Bones and Bobby," the album included his arrangements of three Duke Ellington compositions and the international hit "Getaway" by the highly popular group Earth, Wind and Fire. "Jessica" (Wilson's granddaughter was two years old at the time) featured Ernie Watts on tenor saxophone traversing through three different keys, while "Blues Bones and Bobby" features trumpeter Bobby Bryant in dynamically contrasting solo work, Watts on tenor saxophone, Harold Land Jr. on electric piano, and Milcho Leviev on acoustic piano. Producer Albert Marx, who wrote the liner notes to the LP, notes that Wilson's arrangement of*

> "Getaway," made famous by the superstar group Earth, Wind and Fire, places the orchestra in a modern setting of fusion, funk and soul interspersed with wonderful jazz solos by Oscar Brashear on trumpet, Harold Land, Sr. on tenor sax and Harold Land, Jr. on electric piano.
>
> "Sophisticated Lady," one of the Duke's greatest compositions, fulfills a long time desire of Wilson's to arrange and orchestrate it. This is a vehicle for the tenor sax of Ernie Watts, who indulges, or as the Duke used to say about Harry Carney, "overindulges himself in 'Sophisticated Lady.'"

"Don't Get Around Much Anymore," another fine Ellington composition, spotlights Snooky Young (a colleague of Wilson's since the time they were the two youngest members of the famous Jimmy Lunceford Orchestra) as the main soloist displaying his mastery of the trumpet in an exciting and intense plunger muted solo. Milcho Leviev is very effective with his bluesy and funky solo on synthesizer in the middle of Snooky Young's beautiful work. (ibid.)

Recorded at Mars Studio in November of 1982, musicians on the recording date included the following: Rick Baptist, Hal Espinosa, Oscar Brashear, Eugene "Snooky" Young, Bobby Bryant, trumpets; Ernie Watts, Harold D. Land, Anthony Ortega, Jerome Richardson, Roger Hogan, Hank De Vega, Jack Nimitz, saxophones; Thurman Green, Jimmy Cleveland, Garnett Brown, Maurice Spears, trombones; Harold C. Land, electric piano; Gerald Wiggins, acoustic piano; Milcho Leviev, keyboards; John B. Williams, string and Fender bass; Paul Humphrey, Clayton Cameron, drums; and Jo Villaseñor Wilson, copyist.

Eventually, the Lomelin *and* Jessica *albums would be reissued together as a single CD in 1988, still on the Discovery Records label and billed again as the Gerald Wilson Orchestra of the 80s, this time adopting the title track* Love You Madly.

Wilson would record two more albums on Discovery/Trend Records, Calafia, *recorded in Glendale on November 29–30 in 1984, and* Jenna, *recorded in Hollywood in 1989.* Calafia *included another, and his last, of Wilson's tone poems dedicated to matadors, this time to Eloy Cavazos, born in Guadalupe in the state of Nuevo León, Mexico, and known as "The Little Giant." The title track, "Calafia," has a very significant, historical meaning, as Calafia was the queen of a group of women in a legendary, sixteenth-century story. Spanish explorers named California after her. Also on the LP was "The Redd Foxx," named for the actor/comedian Redd Foxx, for whom Wilson had directed the band for Foxx's NBC live television variety show. Foxx had great commercial success with his previous television show,* Sanford and Son.

Other tracks on the LP included "Polygon," "3/4 for Mayor Tom" (for Los Angeles mayor Tom Bradley), and a new version of "Viva Tirado '85." Musicians on the LP included: Al Aarons, Rick Baptist, Oscar Brashear,

Snooky Young, trumpets; Garnett Brown, Buster Cooper, Thurman Green, Maurice Spears, trombones; Red Callender, tuba; Anthony Ortega, Ernie Watts, Roger Hogan, Harold Land, John Stephens, Henry De Vega, reeds; Milcho Leviev, piano; Stanley Gilbert, bass; and Paul Humphrey, drums.

The LP Jenna: Gerald Wilson's Orchestra of the 90s, *named for another of Wilson's granddaughters, featured the Latin-flavored title track "Jenna," a redone "Carlos," and a number of Wilson's other classics, including "The Wailer," "Blues for Yna Yna," "Yard Dog Mazurka," and "Lunceford Special." Other pieces reflected on the past, e.g., "Back to the Roots," "B-bop and the Song," and "48 Years Later," and the remaining tracks included the jazz standard "Love for Sale," "Margie" (with Snooky Young and Wilson on vocals), and "Flying Home." Personnel included the following: Snooky Young, trumpet and vocals; Raymond Brown, Bob Clark, Rick Baptist, Ron Barrows, Oscar Brashear, trumpets; Thurman Green, Luis Bonilla, Charlie Loper, trombones; Maurice Spears, bass trombone; Danny House, John Stephens, alto saxophones; Louis Taylor, Carl Randall, tenor saxophones; Randall Willis, baritone saxophone; Michael Cain, piano; Anthony Wilson, guitar; Stanley Gilbert, bass; and Mel Lee, drums.*

In 1994, the Gerald Wilson Orchestra was invited as special guests to the Chicago Jazz Festival, performing for 65,000 people. Gary Vercelli notes that Wilson was "grateful for the opportunity to perform before such an appreciative audience. Gerald's band brought the four-day proceeding to a fitting climax in a performance that was made all the more poignant by a birthday celebration in his honor" (Vercelli 1995).

Performing in Chicago was a homecoming of sorts for Wilson, as he had played there as a member of the Jimmie Lunceford, Count Basie, and Dizzy Gillespie orchestras, spent his Navy days stationed there with the Navy Band, and performed there often with his own orchestra, which included vocalist Joe Williams's stint with the band.

Within one year of the festival, Wilson composed and recorded two pieces in homage to the city of Chicago on a new CD released in 1995. The title of "State Street Sweet" (also title track of the CD) was a suggestion of Ruby Rogers, one of the producers of the Chicago Jazz Festival. Vercelli notes that "Wilson wrote this tune to convey the feelings of relaxed tranquility and simultaneous excitement and diversity that imbue this historic Chicago street and its surrounding neighborhoods today" (ibid.). "Lakeshore Drive" features another expanded harmonic scheme incorporating a *melodic theme interpreted by the saxophone section "juxtaposed against syncopated brass and rhythm which together depict the energetic movement on this Chicago thoroughfare that faces beautiful Lake Michigan" (ibid.).*

Featured soloists include pianist Brian O'Rourke (a former student of Wilson's History of Jazz class at California State University, Northridge), Randall Willis on alto saxophone, and Anthony Wilson (Wilson's son) on guitar. Vercelli again comments on Wilson's stylistic innovation, noting that, "the fresh harmonic structures explored here are typical of Wilson's continuing compositional quest to bring on the new" (ibid.).

The CD also featured new recordings of his classic original compositions, including "Lighthouse Blues" (featuring Wilson's son Anthony Wilson and grandson Eric Otis on guitar), "The Serpent" and "The Feather" (both from his Teotihuacán Suite*), "Caprichos," "Jammin' in C," the latter originally written in 1949 for the Count Basie Orchestra, and "Carlos," featuring guest trumpeter Ron Barrows. Also on the recording is Wilson's jazz take of the Neapolitan classic "Come Back to Sorrento," commissioned to Wilson by Leon René and specifically arranged to feature Plas Johnson on tenor saxophone. Vercelli remarks that "here, Gerald's orchestration blends beautifully with the meeting sensuality of Johnson's tenor" (ibid.).*

Personnel on the State Street Sweet *CD, released on the MAMA Foundation label, and recorded at Capitol Studios in Hollywood, included the following: Snooky Young, Bob Clark, Frank Szabo, George Graham, Tony Luján, Bobby Shew, trumpets; John Stevens, Randall Willis, Carl Randall, Louis Taylor, Jack Nimitz, saxophones; Charlie Loper, Ira Nepus, Thurman Green, Alex Iles, Maurice Spears, trombones; Brian O'Rourke, piano; Anthony Wilson, guitar; Trey Henry, bass; Mel Lee, drums; and special guests Plas Johnson, tenor saxophone, Eric Otis, guitar, and Ron Barrows, trumpet.*

In 1996, Wilson recorded Suite Memories: Reflections on a Jazz Journey, *previously referred to extensively in this book. The double-CD set comprises Wilson's spoken word in twenty-four segments and topics representing his life story. Extensive notes were written by Kirk Silsbee for this rich document released through the MAMA Foundation, which has been instrumental in the distribution and preservation of Wilson's classic and new work.*

I feel it is more than worth including here the four testimonials to Wilson printed on the back cover of Suite Memories *by four unique and historically important musicians:*

The world of jazz has been greatly enhanced by the fact that Gerald Wilson decided to work in our arena. Gerald's contributions often don't put him out front, but this unsung hero creates the foundation that the rest of us stand on.
—Ellis Marsalis

As a small boy, I was turned on by Gerald Wilson's compositions "Hi Spook" and "Yard Dog Mazurka," which he recorded with the Lunceford Orchestra. I am still turned on by his current music and band. Gerald should definitely go down in jazz history as one of our great ones—one that has helped build and preserve the foundation of jazz. All praises to Gerald Wilson.
—Horace Silver

Gerald Wilson is a truly fine musician—from the same mold as Ellington, Basie and other greats. As a composer and arranger, he is unique, creative, and always making new music, which is very rare. He is a legend whose music has helped to shape jazz and will do so for a long time to come.
—Buddy Collette

To my ear, there are three great American composers-arrangers: Duke Ellington, Gil Evans, and Gerald Wilson.
—Ray Manzarek, The Doors

It is also essential to include here the words of Wilson himself printed inside the CD jacket:

I would like to extend my warmest thanks to all those who have been important in my journey in jazz:

To all the friends and colleagues mentioned in this album and the countless others not mentioned. To all my teachers—and there have been many. To all those remembered and forgotten, without whose support and guidance I could not have attained the success that I have in jazz. I am deeply indebted to them all for helping me on my path.

To *all* of my family for their enduring love throughout my life. To all the places where I have lived and grown. My hometown Shelby, Mississippi; Memphis, Tennessee; Detroit, Michigan; New York City; Chicago; the Navy base at Great Lakes, Illinois, where I was given the opportunity to write and study music; San Francisco; and my home, Los Angeles.

To everyone at MAMA Foundation for making this project possible. Special thanks to Gene Czerwinski, Connie Czerwinski, Douglas Evans and Armond Bagdasarian.

And finally to God, the greatest bandleader of all, for directing my path and making my life a happy one.

Gerald Wilson
May 1996, Los Angeles

MONTEREY

In 1998, Wilson would work on a recording that would, in many ways, take him back into an intensely creative mode and international profile. The new work and album would also represent a return to the seaport of Monterey, California, where Wilson had performed as part of the Monterey Jazz Festival. That performance followed and inspired Wilson throughout his Pacific Jazz years of the 1960s and into the subsequent decades. Kirk Silsbee wrote the following words to describe this road, to and from Monterey:

1963 was a momentous year for the Monterey Jazz Festival. Modern Jazz, in the form of Miles, Monk, Mulligan and the Modern Jazz Quartet, studded the bill. Clearly, the Monterey Jazz Festival had come of age. Jimmy Lyons, the Festival's founder, had already presented the best of the remaining jazz orchestras from the Golden Age: Duke, Basie, Woody, Harry James. Now, Lyons would indulge his own special passion, big band music, in an important way.

Gerald Wilson, at the cutting edge of jazz orchestration, was given the dominant big band forum that weekend in September. The Los Angeles bandleader whose musical lieutenants included Teddy Edwards, Harold Land, Jack Wilson and Joe Pass, would give the jazz world a message: the future is *this* way.

Riding on the success of its Pacific Jazz albums, the Gerald Wilson Orchestra delivered an object lesson in the possibilities of big band music. Demanding time signatures, multiple key changes, intricate harmonies and, above all, swing, were explored in a new and exciting way. Louis-Victor Mialy, reviewing the Festival for the Paris-based *Jazz* magazine, viewed Wilson's showing as the most exciting thing he'd seen since Dizzy brought his orchestra to France in 1948.

This was the first in a series of distinguished performances by Wilson as a bandleader at the Festival. He would return to score for and direct a Jimmie Lunceford tribute band in 1976. The next year, on its twentieth anniversary, the Festival commissioned Wilson to write the "Happy Birthday Monterey Suite," which he premiered conducting the Air Force Band of Washington, D.C., with guests Clark Terry, Eddie Davis, John Lewis and Mundell Lowe. In 1982, once again Wilson was called in with a commission. His noted Orchestra of the '80s played Wilson's "Lomelin" written for the Festival's Twenty-fifth anniversary, as the climax to an exhilarating midnight concert. (Silsbee 1998)

Nineteen ninety-seven represented the fortieth anniversary of the Monterey Jazz Festival, and the festival director, Tim Jackson, made the decision to commission Wilson to compose a commemorative piece for the occasion. Thus was created Wilson's Theme for Monterey, *a suite in five movements that would emerge as one of Wilson's major works. Silsbee notes that "at its premiere on the closing night of the Festival, the energy on the bandstand and in the crowd was electric. The orchestra delivered an impassioned performance, bringing the entire house to its feet for multiple standing ovations" (ibid.).*

Wilson's first musical encounter with the Monterey Bay and its surrounding, boundless nature and culture was as a trumpet player in Duke Ellington's orchestra in 1960, when the band performed in Carmel. "I'll never forget my first trip to Monterey. The sun was shining. It was warm, bright and beautiful. Then within half an hour it was dark, foggy and drizzling. It's such a beautiful place, that it's easy to draw inspiration from" (ibid.).

Four of the suite's five movements are inspired by the 17-Mile Drive and the Spanish Bay, Carmel-by-the-Sea, the Lone Cypress Tree near the coast, and Cannery Row. In describing his main message, Wilson commented, "In my recent works, I've stayed away from some of the symphonic devices I've used elsewhere. I want this music to swing in any tempo, even the ballads." For Theme for Monterey, *he "wanted the theme to ring in the listener's ears long after we finished playing. I wanted them to walk away swinging and humming the tune. After all, this is jazz, and everything must swing!" (ibid.)*

Theme for Monterey *became the title track for the 1998 album produced by the MAMA Foundation on its MAMA Records label. Significant to the project and germane to Wilson's role in education and jazz history are the goals of the MAMA Foundation, printed on the CD jacket as follows:*

1. Preservation of the music of culturally significant vocal and instrumental artists whose work does not have large commercial appeal.

2. Distribution of these works to schools, universities, libraries, and the general public.

3. Provision of financial support and technical assistance to vocal and instrumental artists in their experimental works.

Albums produced by MAMA Foundation are donated to a select group of schools, museums, and archives, as well as being offered through the normal distribution channels to the general public. Funds generated from these sales are used to help support the preservation and sharing of music that otherwise might be lost forever.

Also included in the CD are Wilson's arrangements of "Summertime" from George and Ira Gershwin's opera Porgy and Bess *in addition to "Anthropology," a classic bebop tune by Dizzy Gillespie, Charlie Parker,* and Walter Bishop Jr. These arrangements were commissioned in 1996 by the Ira and Leonore Gershwin Foundation, and were premiered at Lincoln Theatre in Washington, DC, for a Library of Congress gala honoring the initial archiving of Wilson's music. The inclusion of "Anthropology" pays homage to the fact that the harmonic changes adapted to the tune were those composed by George Gershwin in his "I Got Rhythm," also from Porgy and Bess.

Soloists featured on the Theme for Monterey CD included Scott Mayo on soprano and alto saxophone; Louis Taylor, soprano saxophone; Anthony Wilson, guitar; Oscar Brashear, Ron Barrows, Carl Saunders, trumpets; Carl Randall, Randall Willis, tenor saxophones; George Bohanon, Isaac Smith, trombones; and Brian O'Rourke, piano. Recorded in November of 1997 at Capitol Studios in Hollywood, the complete orchestra personnel on the album, aside from the soloists above, included the following musicians: Snooky Young, David Krimsley, trumpets; Leslie Benedict, Maurice Spears, trombones; John Stephens, Jack Nimitz, saxophones; Eric Otis, guitar; Trey Henry, bass; and Mel Lee, drums.

In 2003, Wilson was invited by drummer/producer and alumnus of the Jazz Crusaders, Stix Hooper, to record an album in New York City with an assemblage of New York-based musicians. The CD, New York, New Sound, features many of the top jazz artists in the city, including Clark Terry, Jon Faddis, Jimmy Owens, Frank Greene, and Sean Jones on trumpet, Benny Powell, Luis Bonilla, Dennis Wilson, Douglas Wilson, and Douglas Purviance on trombone, Jimmy Heath, Frank Wess, Jesse Davis, Jerry Dodgion, and Jay Brandford on reeds, Kenny Barron and Renee Rosnes on piano, Anthony Wilson and Oscar Castro-Nieves on guitar, Larry Ridley, Trey Henry, and Bob Cranshaw on bass, Lewis Nash and Stix Hooper on drums, and Lenny Castro on Latin percussion.

The repertoire recorded comprised eight of Wilson's classic compositions in addition to his classic arrangements of John Coltrane's "Equinox" and Miles Davis's "Milestones." His originals included "Blues for the Count," "Viva Tirado," "Teri," "Blues for Yna Yna," "Theme for Monterey," "M Capetillo," "Josefina," and "Nancy Jo." Testimonials were printed inside the CD jacket by Clark Terry, Kenny Barron, Benny Powell, Jimmy Heath, Frank Wess, Renee Rosnes, Anthony Wilson, Jon Faddis, Jimmy Owens, and Lewis Nash. The album was nominated for a Grammy Award.

In 2005, Wilson recorded his second album on the Mack Avenue label, In My Time. *The recording was his second with what he was now referring to as his New York band, which included most of the musicians that had recorded on his first Mack Avenue Records New York orchestra CD in 2003,* New York, New Sound. In My Time *also revisited some of Wilson's classic compositions and/or arrangements, including "Lomelin," featuring Jon Faddis on trumpet, "Sax Chase," "Musette," "So What" (Miles Davis), "Love for Sale" (Cole Porter), and "Jeri."*

"a. e. n." is a minor blues composition that Wilson dedicated to his son, Anthony, and his grandsons, Eric and Nicholas. The arrangement features solos by Renee Rosnes (piano), Kamasi Washington (tenor saxophone), Jimmy Owens (trumpet), Steve Wilson (alto saxophone), Russell Malone (guitar), and Jeremy Pelt (trumpet).

The Diminished Triangle *is a suite of three movements titled "Dorian," "Ray's Vision at the U," and "Blues for Manhattan." Ray Briggs, a professor of music and associate director of the jazz studies program at California State University, Long Beach, and vice president of the California Institute for the Preservation of Jazz, wrote the liner notes for* In My Time, *in which he described the commissioning of the suite.*

The California Institute for the Preservation of Jazz, which had honored many jazz greats posthumously during its annual festivals in the past, wanted to focus on a significant contributor to jazz that was nonetheless still alive. After being selected and accepting the invitation to participate in the CIPJ Spring Festival of 2005, Wilson was commissioned to compose a multi-movement work supported by a generous grant from the National Endowment for the Arts. That extended-composition titled "The Diminished Triangle" was premiered on April 2, 2005. That overwhelmingly successful performance is captured in the full-length studio recording heard on this CD. . . .

In addition to his studiousness and commitment, Wilson is a creative genius. He firmly believes that to remain true to the spirit of jazz, one must create new art. Whether in creating a unique style influenced by his interest in the art of bullfighting (e.g. the mega-hit "Viva Tirado" and the recently recorded "Lomelin"), or composing works, such as "5/21/72," commissioned by the Los Angeles Philharmonic under the direction of Zubin Mehta and later performed by both the New York and the Israel Philharmonic Orchestras, Wilson has always moved on to explore territory.

The tracks [here] are simply a continuation of that search for new territory and demonstrative of Wilson's mastery of jazz harmony, arranging, and skill in leading a band. As many great arrangers have attested, the musicians in the band "make the sound." Here the maestro has surrounded himself with the best possible mix of seasoned veterans. (Briggs 2005)

When I first heard the In My Time *CD, I felt that the recorded performance could very well be the tightest ever released of Wilson's orchestras. His compositions and arrangements are played at the highest level of precision, dynamics, and artistic interpretation. My feelings about this epic recording were reinforced—or, shall I say, even vindicated—when I later read a review of the CD by Ron Saranich, in which Wilson is quoted as saying, "I've listened to* In My Time *several times and, honestly, this might be the best record I've ever made. The intonation of the musicians is so good, the musicians interpreted the music so well, and they are great young players who are looking ahead, moving the banner of jazz into the future" (Saranich 2005).*

Personnel on the recording included the following: Jon Faddis, Frank Greene, Jimmy Owens, Jeremy Pelt, Eddie Henderson, Mike Rodríguez, Sean Jones, trumpets; Benny Powell, Dennis Wilson, Douglas Purviance, Luis Bonilla, trombones; Kamasi Washington, Gary Smulyan, Ron Blake, Steve Wilson, Jerry Dodgion, Dustin Cicero, reeds; Russell Malone, guitar; Lewis Nash, drums; Peter Washington, upright bass; and Renee Rosnes, piano.

It should be noted, as the title indicates, that the second movement of the suite is dedicated to Professor Briggs, who notes that the "three movement work explores the harmonic possibilities of the three diminished chords." Briggs also comments that "as for the compositions particular attention should be paid to 'Jeri,' which is named for Wilson's first-born daughter and the harmonic foundation of the entire album according to the composer."

The year 2006 represented another important milestone for Wilson. The Jazz at Lincoln Center organization in New York City produced a series of concerts celebrating the jazz cities of America, and dedicated one to Gerald Wilson and tenor saxophonist Plas Johnson entitled Los Angeles: Central Avenue Breakdown. *Featured in the concert was the Jazz at Lincoln Center Orchestra led by Wynton Marsalis at Frederick P. Rose Hall on Broadway and Sixtieth Street in New York City. Wilson conducted the orchestra for the concert, which performed a program of his compositions and arrangements.*

In 2007, Wilson received another commission from the Monterey Jazz Festival to compose a suite he titled Monterey Moods. *He recorded it in the same year, again on the Mack Avenue Records label, and again with his New York-based band, similar in personnel to that of his 2003* New York, New Sound *recording. The new suite consisted of nine movements: "Allegro," "Jazz Swing Waltz," "Ballad," "Latin Swing," "Blues Bass Solo," "Hard Swing," "I Concentrate on You" (a reinterpretation of the Cole Porter standard), and "The Mini-Waltz." Featured as a guest soloist was virtuoso flutist Hubert Laws, while the orchestra included frontline musicians such as Jon Faddis, Terrell Stafford, Jimmy Owens, Sean Jones, Dennis Wilson, Kamasi Washington, Steve Wilson, Antonio Hart, Ron Blake, Renee Rosnes, Peter Washington, Lewis Nash, and Anthony Wilson. The album was produced by Al Pryer, and its liner notes included the following testimonials:*

> Gerald Wilson's longevity with his creativity alone gives testimony to his value as an international treasure. To participate with Gerald and the wonderful young talented players on this project was a highlight and education for me.
> —Hubert Laws

> Playing with Gerald Wilson is always such a joy and an inspiration, as is hearing the results. Listening, of course, you'll find swingin' music; you'll also discover Gerald Wilson the person . . . intelligent, wise, full of joy and classy, just like his compositions.
> —Jon Faddis

Gerald Wilson is one of the greatest composers and arrangers living today. For decades, he has been in the upper echelon of creative artists. His latest work, *Monterey Moods*, is another example
of his genius.

—Kenny Burrell

In 2009, Wilson's CD entitled Detroit *was released on Mack Avenue
Records, his fourth on the label. The recording's title composition is a
six-part suite commissioned by the Detroit International Jazz Festival in
celebration of its thirtieth anniversary. Of great significance to the commission was Wilson's relationship to the city of Detroit, having lived there
during his high school years (1934–39) where he attended Cass Tech and
for which he titled the suite's second movement. In the CD's liner notes,
Wilson is quoted as saying, "Detroit, it's home to me, one of my homes,
anyway . . . I had wanted to live in the North, so the day I arrived in
Detroit, staying with family friends, was a day I had dreamed of. Unlike
other places I had lived, Detroit was integrated. So, for me, Detroit was
freedom" (Stewart 2009).*

*Stewart notes that "for the suite, Gerald employs his expansive har-
monic concept, where he can get up to 10 different voices for a given chord,
resulting in vibrant walls of sound" (ibid.). The first movement is described
by Wilson as "a blues number. Blues are the backbone of jazz." He titled
the movement "Belle Isle" after a beautiful park on the Detroit River. The
second movement, "Cass Tech," is subtitled "Variations on a Theme by
B.G.," coding the fact that it is constructed on the theme and chord changes
to Benny Golson's "Along Came Betty." The third movement, "Detroit," is
a ballad that Stewart describes as "Wilson's love song to the city" (ibid.).
Featured are Randall Willis on flute and Kamasi Washington on tenor
saxophone. Wilson notes that "the two notes of the theme actually say
'De-troit' . . . Here, I'm trying to catch people's ears with some beautiful music for a beautiful, magnificent city" (ibid.). "Miss Gretchen," the
suite's fourth movement, is dedicated to Gretchen Valade, Mack Avenue
Records' owner and executive producer, whom Wilson describes as "a very
alive, wonderful person" (ibid.). The movement is also a tribute to Billy
Strayhorn, "drawing on his classic 'Chelsea Bridge' for some harmonic
movement. Ben Webster's solo on the song's bridge, from an Ellington
recording, is played by violinist Yvette Devereaux" (Stewart, ibid.).*

Of particular interest in the suite is the fifth movement, "Before Mo-town," as it is constructed on the patented Wilson use of Latin/Spanish forms, again referencing the paso doble *intersected with a highly progressive harmonic structure and anticipated Afro-Cuban bass lines. Especially provocative is Wilson's concluding chorus of deeply layered and harmonically expansive, full-orchestra voicing. Another dynamically up-tempo blues piece comprises the sixth and final movement, titled "The Detroit River," which Wilson refers to as "kind of a wild thing" (ibid.).*

In addition to *Detroit*, the CD also features additional pieces by Wilson, recorded previously in 2007 with Wilson's New York band. These include "Everywhere" and "Aram," the latter originally recorded on Wilson's *Portraits* album on Pacific Jazz. As the suite *Detroit* was recorded in Los Angeles, the CD consists of the following sets of orchestra personnel: Los Angeles: Ron Barrows, Bobby Rodríguez, Jeff Kaye, Rick Baptist, Winston Byrd, trumpets; Carl Randall, Jackie Kelso, Kamasi Washington, Louis Van Taylor, Randall Willis, Terry Landry, reeds; Eric Jorgensen, Les Benedict, Mike Wimberly, Shaunte Palmer, trombones; Yvette Devereaux, violin; Brian O'Rourke, piano; Mel Lee, drums; Trey Henry, bass; Sean Jones, guest trumpet; Anthony Wilson, guest guitar. New York: Jon Faddis, Frank Greene, Sean Jones, Jimmy Ownes, Terrell Stafford, trumpets/flugelhorns; Steve Wilson, Antonio Hart, Ron Blake, Kamasi Washington, Ronnie Cuber, reeds; Dennis Wilson, Luis Bonilla, Jay Ashby, Douglas Purviance, trombones; Lewis Nash, drums; Renee Rosnes, piano; Peter Washington, bass; Anthony Wilson, guitar; Todd Coolman, bass; and Hubert Laws, guest flute.

An interesting and richly expressive line was printed on the back cover of the advance copy of the Detroit *CD, and I feel it merits printing it here also: "*Detroit *is a six-part suite that evokes both the edge and the ambition of this blue collar city. An iconic Big Band composer, arranger and leader, Gerald gathers his bi-coastal roster of musicians together into one true House of Jazz."*

In 2011, Mack Avenue Records released what may be Wilson's most eclectic album. Legacy *was yet another salute to Chicago with the inclusion of Wilson's newly penned, seven-movement* Yes Chicago Is . . . *(Suite). But the recording also included five other pieces, three inspired by European classical composers and the other two composed by his son, Anthony, and grandson Eric. Ninety-two years old at the time of the recording, Wilson was profiled in the liner notes by Neil Tesser as follows:*

> Albums such as *State Street Sweet, Monterey Moods* and now *Legacy*—all created after his 75th birthday—have further bolstered that legacy, at an age when most guys just buy a new recliner and bask in old glories. (Tesser 2011)

Yes Chicago Is . . . *was the second commission awarded to Wilson after the first in 1994 (resulting in* State Street Suite*) by the Chicago Jazz Festival. Wilson debuted the suite at the 2008 festival, in what became his second major homage to the city of Chicago. Tesser describes the suite as comprising "seven short movements based on the same melody, with changes in color, harmony, tempo and tone providing the variety" (ibid.). Wilson explained the concepts of these seven movements and their titles:*

> Right at the top, we know Chicago was "A Jazz Mecca." I wanted to say, musically, what a beautiful thing it is to walk down Michigan Avenue. Then comes "A Night at El Grotto," . . . [a] club where we played 10 weeks in 1946. Now we go "Riffin' At the Regal," the Regal Theater, which was next to the Savoy Ballroom, where all the big bands played. It's kind of an up-tempo thing, because I had in mind the jitney cabs that ran up and down South Parkway. . . . "Cubs, Bears, Bulls, and White Sox" was titled for Chicago's Sports teams. (ibid.)

Wilson named "47th St. Blues" for the historic street of legendary blues clubs; "Blowin' in the Windy City" is his recollection of the exciting and busy Chicago scene of the 1940s.

In his "Variation on a Theme by Igor Stravinsky," Wilson develops ideas inspired by Stravinsky's The Firebird *suite. He initiates the piece with a novel set of melodies echoing Stravinsky's melodies and modernist themes, following with some rich orchestration based on a harmonic syncopation of the three horn sections, as well as subsequent improvisation by members of the band. "Variations on Clair de Lune" represents a more direct use of the principle theme of its source, in this case the piano classic "Clair de Lune" by Claude Debussy. Wilson set the melodic theme within a serene orchestration of the full ensemble, constructed on a tight blues feel and scheme. Rich voicings again characterize Wilson's unique and always progressive approach. An up-tempo, straight-ahead swing section of a refreshing chord progression features well developed and heartfelt solo improvisations on alto saxophone, trumpet, and piano. A return to the blues feel closes the piece.*

With his "Variation On a Theme by Giacomo Puccini" ("Nessun Dorma" from the opera Turandot), *Wilson adapts the popular vocal melody to a lyrically following trumpet introduction, allowing for an improvisatory approach to the legato, sentimental theme. An up-tempo solo section follows, featuring trumpet and baritone saxophone, ultimately returning to the serenity of the principal theme on trumpet.*

"Virgo" is a composition and arrangement by Anthony Wilson. The piece opens with serene solo piano figurations responded to by a main theme on trumpet underlying the slow tempo theme. There is diverse, highly sophisticated scoring throughout, with both a combination of rich harmonic structures and nicely balanced counterpoint in the horn sections. The theme shifts to an up-tempo section featuring Wilson's guitar improvisation, which is followed by a more orchestral interplay on a set of nicely fluid chord changes, and a dynamic alto saxophone solo. All the while, complex yet beautifully interwoven orchestral variations are heard underneath.

"September Sky" is another beautifully written and scored composition, this time composed by Eric Otis. A ballad-type theme is introduced on flute, followed by improvisation on the theme. The same format is repeated on flugelhorn, segueing into an up-tempo tenor saxophone solo, supported by tight and keen orchestration below. Piano figurations, which began the piece, end it in serene fashion.

Both Anthony Wilson and Eric Otis demonstrate some remarkable abilities as composers and orchestrators. They both echo through their bloodline and closeness to Wilson the same rich harmonic, textural, and contrapuntal innovations that he has set into practice for so many years and so much writing. Tesser provides a very telling narrative of this family working relationship and closeness:

"Virgo" comes from Gerald's son Anthony, a splendid and lyrical guitarist and also a gifted composer-arranger in his own right. And

Gerald's heritage now extends to another generation: "September Sky" was written by his grandson, Eric Otis.

"He's literally my eyes and hands," explains Wilson; macular degeneration has left him unable to copy down his own music. "So I sit at the piano and I tell him everything to write. I call out, 'First trumpet A, dotted eighth' [i.e., the pitch, the rhythm and the instrument playing it] and Eric puts it all down."

I can't imagine a more time-consuming way to compose a big-band chart: note by note, instrument by instrument. But I also can't imagine a more clear image of handing down the family craft from one generation to another—or a better example of the legacy that Gerald Wilson conveys on this most appropriately titled album. (Tesser 2011)

CHAPTER 7

THE LATIN DIMENSION OF GERALD WILSON

You like all kinds of music, Mingus? I was born in Key West, Florida. My family's Cuban.
You play Cuban music?" "I'm not hip to that, Fats. I know some Mexican tunes."
—CHARLES MINGUS

In 1948, Wilson met and was soon married to Josefina Villaseñor. In 2013, they celebrated more than sixty years of marriage. They were blessed with three children, Geraldine (Jeri), Lillian (Teri), and Nancy Jo, and as noted in chapter 5, Wilson titled compositions after each of them. He also titled pieces after his son, Anthony, and all of his grandchildren. Teri, who married Shuggie Otis, an important guitarist and son of legendary musician Johnny Otis, passed away in 2001. The importance of family, especially as it plays a major role in Latin American and African American culture, has in many ways sculpted the artistic and spiritual profile of Gerald Wilson.

Wilson's marriage to Josefina not only changed his personal life but also changed much of the cultural context that had always been such an essential element in his artistic enculturation and creative approach and output: Josefina was of Mexican heritage. The daughter of parents originally from Jalisco, Mexico, she grew up in a bilingual, bicultural setting in the Los Angeles area. The children of Wilson and Josefina would have an African American and Mexican heritage, and this duality would begin to emerge in Wilson's music. I remember Wilson once telling me that Josefina would often remind him that his Latin music influence came from her.

It was during the 1950s that Wilson developed a special affinity for the art of bullfighting. He and his wife began to make trips to Tijuana, Mexico, two hours south of Los Angeles, to attend bullfights at the Plaza Monumental, the Tijuana bullring. Bullfighting had been part of Josefina's Mexican culture, especially since her parents were from the state of Jalisco in Mexico, where bullfighting had an important presence in many of the cities and small towns.

Inspired by the art, pageantry, and improvisatory styles of the individual matadors, Wilson began to follow as an avid aficionado, and initiated a series of tone poems in the jazz idiom dedicated to these artists. However, these compositions were characterized by concepts and patterns derived from traditional Spanish, Mexican, and Cuban musical genres. Wilson made use of the rhythmic, harmonic, and melodic nuances of forms in-cluding the paso doble *(often identified with the bullfight),* habanera, canción, bolero, cha cha chá, mambo, *in addition to the compositional elements of Spanish and Latin American symphonic composers. (Some of these stylizations and influences are covered in chapters 5 and 6.)*

This "Latin dimension" of Gerald Wilson is thus personified through an extensive list of his compositions, some of which represent his most acclaimed and signature pieces. A good number of these pieces, of course, have been dedicated to bullfighters, while others exploit different Latin themes. This list is characterized by the following compositions and ar-rangements: "Viva Tirado," "Carlos," "Latino," "Paco," "Caprichos," "Los Moros de España," "El Viti," "Ricardo," Teotihuacán Suite, *"Chanson du Feu Follet," "Blues Latinese," "Man of La Mancha," "Del Olivar,"* "M. Capetillo," "El Presidente," and "Lomelin."*

There have also been other compositions and arrangements by Wilson intoned by popular forms in Latin America, as with the boleros popular-ized by Mexican-based groups and singers such as Trio Los Panchos and Javier Solís. One such example was the bolero "La Mentira," composed by Alvaro Carrillo, for which Wilson adapted the bolero rhythm and tone in a richly original instrumental arrangement for his orchestra. Conversely, he also composed an original number molded in the bolero form, "Mi Corazón."

Another highly significant aspect of Wilson's Latin dimension has been his consistent employment of Latino musicians in his orchestra, especially Mexican Americans, who represent the majority of Latinos in Los Angeles.

The list of these Latino artists is a considerable and impressive one, includ-ing the likes of Anthony Ortega, Ray Bojórquez, Henry De Vega, Ruben McFall, Hal Espinoza, Alex Rodríguez, Bobby Rodríguez, Tony Luján, Modesto Durán, Harold Land Jr., and Luis Bonilla, among others.

VIVA TIRADO

"Viva Tirado," to many, Wilson's most acclaimed and popular signature piece, has symbolized not only Wilson's absorption of the Latin culture, its style and spirit, but also its contexts of social expression and political change. In the interviews we conducted, I asked Wilson some specific questions about his composition of "Viva Tirado," and how that tune emerged as such a powerful musical symbol in the Mexican American, or Chicano, community.

Loza: Gerald, we have discussed the whole issue of . . . how you had written the suite for the bullfighting themes . . . how you'd gotten into the themes of Mexico and Spain, and then how one of those tunes was adopted by El Chicano that became a big popular hit (1970), and then years later even became a hip-hop hit with Kid Frost. And it's funny, because with that tune, "Viva Tirado" . . . I was in Chicago recently and I remember . . . a professor at the University of Illinois saying, "Have you ever heard of a group called El Chicano?" Of course, he knew them because of that tune. And I said, "Know them?" "Do you know about the guy who wrote the tune?" I told him the whole story. Of course, a lot of that is in my book *Barrio Rhythm*. And it became a hit for the Chicano movement. In the PBS special on the history of the Chicano civil rights movement, "Viva Tirado" is one of the principal themes for the whole documentary. So have you thought about the effect that tune has had, not just musically, but socially, even politically? It became an anthem of the Chicano movement. Have you thought about that?
Wilson: Sure, I've thought about it many times. I've thought of the fact that first of all it was dedicated to a fine young matador that I had the honor and pleasure of meeting, José Ramón Tirado. And he was very happy about it. He liked it, which made me feel good. And then when the El Chicano group picked it up they were into the kind of the rock thing

that was going at that time. And they did very well with it in *Billboard*. I think it got to be no. 2, if I'm not mistaken. So naturally that makes it one of the good numbers of the time. In fact, I have a citation and an award from BMI with [it as] one of the biggest songs of the sixties. It's very nice. I can thank El Chicano for what they did. But as you say, socially too it makes it a good thing because it shows that music can bring people together. Jazz music . . . not just jazz music, but music within itself can bring people together. I've thought about it many, many times.

Loza: That tune, to use a musical cliché, hit a "chord" with the Chicano and Latino community and probably the black community and probably the white community. Everybody listened to it. It was sort of like Tito Puente's "Oye Como Va" that Santana did. The same thing happened. Santana took the tune of a bandleader, but Tito Puente. And about this same time period, about 1970 when El Chicano did "Viva Tirado." Santana did "Oye Como Va" [which, along with other hits, catapulted him as the innovative leader of "Latin rock"]. He might have gotten the idea from El Chicano. So El Chicano took a bandleader, Gerald Wilson's tune, and then Santana took Tito Puente's tune, "Oye Como Va"; they were both sort of like simple riff cha-cha type rhythms and they transformed them into more of a rock format, the same process. And these two tunes are literally the two tunes that became the anthems. And then what happens is another twenty years go by and the hip-hoppers pick up both tunes. "Oye Como Va" was made into hip-hop, but the one that really got over was when they took "Viva Tirado" from El Chicano. Kid Frost took it and made it the underlay on a tune called "La Raza." Now, that's a very political, socially charged thing. "La Raza," when he's talking about being proud of being *La Raza*, but he's also talking about this macho fighting, which is in a way a bit absurd but there was another layer of meaning to the tune and it was the pride . . . being a Chicano, Mexican, Latino. And I think that the real reason that this struck a chord was because the musical fusion of jazz and let's say, Latin music, is really in a way what a lot of Chicanos, especially here in LA, were about. You were talking about your neighborhood today, which is mostly inhabited by African Americans and Mexicans and Latinos. So the music reflects again that experience, the mixing, what we call *mestizaje*. We just met your granddaughter, who's part African American Creole, which can mean part French, and Mexican because of your wife, and she's a beautiful woman.

THE SOCIAL AND CULTURAL EFFECTS OF "VIVA TIRADO"

In his book Chicano Soul: Recordings and History of an American Culture, *Ruben Molina notes that "like the enormously talented ground-
breaking San Francisco Bay Area group Santana, El Chicano helped to
open the door for a growing number of west coast musicians that were
already headed down the Latin rock/Latin jazz path. In several ways
"Viva Tirado" was pivotal in creating this new sound that would become
synonymous with East Los Angeles" (Molina 2007: 118).*

*El Chicano, originally the VIPs, began rehearsing in the Los Angeles
suburb of San Gabriel, led by bassist Freddie Sanchez. In 1968, the group
added a horn section consisting of trumpeter Bobby Loya and tenor saxophonist Tony Garcia. Molina (76) quotes the group's guitarist, Mickey
Lespron, who recalled that "it was Bobby Loya who introduced us to jazz
and 'Viva Tirado' which was performed by the horns at the break [of club
dates, etc.]." Loya described the episode as follows:*

> With the VIPs we were doing a lot of rhythm and blues. We had
> Clarence Playa singing Wilson Picket stuff . . . Then I got a thrill
> when I went to the Lighthouse in Hermosa Beach to see trumpeter
> Gerald Wilson. That was a big, big Afro-American jazz band and I
> listened to them perform "Viva Tirado" and then I went and bought
> the album "Moment of Truth" and I thought "Man that's a good
> tune," maybe I can talk Freddie Sanchez into playing it. I thought
> the VIPs were just a typical rock 'n' roll band from the San Gabriel
> Valley so when I introduced "Viva Tirado" I was shocked when
> Freddie Sanchez said, "Yea! Let's do this." I suggested that we bring
> in a percussionist and start doing some Mongo Santamaría. He
> liked that idea too, so little by little we started to change the cata-
> log from the Wilson Pickett and Otis Redding stuff that Clarence
> Playa was singing to more of a Latin jazz feel. It just evolved into
> something different and with Mickey Lespron getting into the Wes
> Montgomery style of playing it just added a different dimension to it.
> (Molina 77)[2]

---

2. Reyes and Waldman (2009), incorporating an interview with El Chicano organist Bobby
Espinoza, provide more detail concerning the recording and nationwide aftermath of "Viva
Tirado."

In another important book examining Chicano music, Chicano Rap: Gender and Violence in the Postindustrial Barrio, *Pancho McFarland essentialized the significance of rapper Kid Frost's "La Raza," constructed over the framework of El Chicano's recording of Gerald Wilson's "Viva Tirado":*

> I first heard Kid Frost in 1990. His first single off of his first LP, *Hispanic Causing Panic* (1990), was "La Raza." In the late 1980s, many of the members of The Colorado College's Chicana/o student group, MEChA, listened to rap music, but no one we heard was rapping about the Chicana/o experience. So, at our parties when we wanted to stir up Chicana/o pride, we played Santana or Los Lobos. "La Raza" became our theme song, and upon hearing the instrumental opening of the song, a sample of "Viva Tirado" by one of our favorite groups, El Chicano, everyone at MEChA parties would run to the dance floor. "La Raza" inevitably kicked our parties into higher levels of fun, pride, and sexuality (McFarland 2008: 35).
>
> The MEChistas were dancing to the polyrhythmic syncopated beats characteristic of the African diaspora. The rhythmic structures of Frost's music, as well as that of Santana and the blues of Los Lobos, result from our very long history of living in close proximity to and exchanging worldviews and culture with African Americans. (36)

It is not mere coincidence that the life and music of Gerald Wilson has been so ingrained with Mexican/Latino culture. In addition to marrying and raising a family with a Mexican American, his work as a bandleader and composer has transpired most of his professional life in Los Angeles, a city and county that has grown into a population of over 50 percent Latino.

Gaye Johnson notes that "for as long as they have occupied common living and working spaces, African American and Chicano working-class communities have had continuous interactions around civil rights struggles, union activism, and demographic changes" (2002: 316). Mexicans and blacks have especially lived side by side in the low-rent housing of south central Los Angeles, and music via radio and the streets has a prolific interchange of value and understanding.

Since the 1930s, radio stations have broadcasted swing music to a multiracial public, and Matt Garcia (1998) has written about the 1930–50s dancehall promoters in Los Angeles who showcased swing, zoot suit styles, and early rock 'n' roll at dances comprising young Mexican, black, Filipino, and white working-class fans. Garcia observed that "the racial/ ethnic intermixing facilitated a blending of cultural influences," and that the ensuing music "possessed a broad-based, cross-cultural appeal, which facilitated understanding among a racially diverse audience" (163). Garcia also noted that interracial dating was another consequence of this positive context. McFarland notes that "such multicultural youth interaction in the middle part of the twentieth century resulted in a process of cultural exchange and borrowing that birthed lowrider culture, rock and roll music, and contemporary gang and street culture" (2008: 36). McFarland adds a final testimony to Kid Frost and his connection to the legacy of Gerald Wilson:

> Kid Frost was the first Chicano to have a successful widely released rap album. The "Godfather of Latin Rap" was the first to bring the beats, attitude, and lyricism of rap to many Chicana/o audiences. His unapologetic *raza* pride and barrio tales rapped over hard beats and familiar samples from oldies and Chicano groups such as El Chicano and Malo opened the door for many Chicana/o youths to participate in rap and hip-hop culture. Since his first release, Kid Frost (now Frost) has released more than a dozen albums, greatest hits collections, and mix tapes. His music and career exemplify African American-Chicana/o cultural exchange.
>
> His first hit, the song that MEChistas danced to during the early 1990s, "La Raza," uses the El Chicano interpolation of African American composer Gerald Wilson's "[Viva] Tirado." (37–38)

Finally, yet another point of view on the seminal role of "Viva Tirado" emerges from Rafael Pérez-Torres in his book Mestizaje: Critical Uses of Race in Chicano Culture:

> Although oftentimes ignored by mainstream history, cultural memory serves to evoke a historical conscious counternarrative. Kid Frost's use of the popular El Chicano's "Viva Tirado" evokes the Chicano movement, that moment of great political and social activism among Chicano populations in the late 1960s and early

1970s. From the affirmation of Brown Power to the Blowouts (high school protests in East Los Angeles), this period represented a high-water mark in the struggle by Americans of Mexican descent for civil rights and political engagement. The musical evocations of the group El Chicano serve both to index and to evoke this period of subaltern resistance. (95)

As reflected through the writers cited above, the concept of mestizaje, *the mixing of race and culture, plays into the matrix of Latino-African American relations. In the* culture *part of this equation, the "mixture," or intersection of shared and learned behavior, can be enacted through musical styles, ideologies, religion, and emotions, among many other spaces of human experience. Musical forms—such as the Mexican son, those of the marimba, and the danzón in Mexico City (by way of Cuba)—are prime examples of this, and inhabit the spaces mentioned above, evoking African as much as indigenous and Spanish heritages. The same can be said about what were originally various regional forms developed among Latinos in the US, such as salsa, Latin jazz, Latin rock, and bugalú. All of these forms inhabit the spaces of racial and cultural interlife, and inhabit the spaces of musical style, ideology, emotions, and the spirit.*

CHAPTER 8

FROM A MUSICAL POINT OF VIEW
Musical Philosophy and Style

Strict musical analysis of jazz . . . is also as limited as a
means of jazz criticism as a strict sociological approach.
—LEROI JONES (AMIRI BARAKA)

*Putting into perspective much of the biographical and musical data that I
have surveyed thus far, one of the most salient features of Gerald Wilson's
music is that of innovation. It is important to note that Wilson's innovative
character is not limited to his constantly evolving musical style but also
to his creative relationships to cultural traditions (many outside the jazz
world, to the media), racial integration, education, and the performance
context.*

*Wilson's pilgrimage has been, from the outset, a search for new things
and new ideas. As told in the previous "Moment of Truth" chapter, Wilson
left the music business at the apex of his early career. He did so because
he was still searching for a musical identity and expertise that still eluded
him. This would happen again in various forms, and these moments in
his pilgrimage have largely defined his musical philosophy and style.*

*One important note should be made here: the following musical
readings, as with the work of Wilson previously reviewed in this book,
are largely based on recordings of the music. This means that live performance, out of which emerges jazz and most other music throughout
history, is not really the major focus of this analysis. Travis A. Jackson
probes this issue extensively in his recent book* Blowin' the Blues Away:

Performance and Meaning in the New York Jazz Scene *(2012). The restrictions of the recording studio, the selected repertoire, and the variations and variety of recording equipment, producers, and engineers all add to questions of how we rely so much on the recording to study a music that is mostly performed live and for audiences.*

But Gerald Wilson represents yet another anomaly in terms of jazz culture and the music industry. Wilson has for many years made it clear that his band does not rely on rehearsals, and that when he records he wants to keep the music as spontaneous as possible. This certainly does not equate into his recordings matching his live performance in experience, effect, or executions, for better or worse; however, he has always felt that he comes close.

And we have other contexts to consider besides the musical performance and the recording. For one thing, Wilson's conducting style—in many senses, a full-body choreography of musical direction—deserves a whole chapter here in terms of its effect not only on the audience but on the musicianship and expressive interpretation of his orchestra. The conducting styles of Ellington, Calloway, and Mehta can be compared and consolidated with that of Wilson, who does so many things that no one—including that trio—has ever done or attempted.

Another context is that of the musical arrangement, the score. Wilson has produced meticulous scores for most of his compositions and arrangements, but he has allowed these blueprints to be adhered and adopted to the context at hand, whether it be changing personnel, diverse performance venues, uniquely talented soloists or section musicians, or spontaneous decisions in live or studio performances. For Wilson, his scores are not a destination—they are part of his pilgrimage.

Yet another context that also defines Wilson's musical style is the concept of the orchestra as his instrument. Wilson certainly inherited and learned this role from mentors such as Basie and Ellington. But it is the role of Ellington especially, as both musical director and physically expressive conductor, that perhaps pervades in this area of Wilson's relationship to his orchestra. In his classic The Jazz Tradition, *Martin Williams, describing Ellington, sounded as he could also be profiling Wilson.*

Ellington's works were produced in an atmosphere of improvisation and experiment. The solos usually came from the soloists, and, as alternate "takes" and the surviving broadcast versions con-firm, the players were free to stick to them from one performance to the next. They were also free to reinterpret and ornament them, and—depending on the context and if so moved—to reject them and come up with new solos.

All the great Ellington works depend on a relationship between soloist and group, between what is written (or perhaps merely memorized) and what may be extemporized, between the individual part and the total effect, and a relationship among beginning, middle, and end. A great Ellington performance is not a series of brilliant episodes but a whole greater than the sum of its parts. He learned how to discipline improvisation and extend orchestration—to the enhancement of both. (Williams 1993: 101–102)

Williams also makes another observation, apt to both Ellington and Gerald Wilson: "Ellington refined jazz beyond the achievements of anyone else. He orchestrated and enriched its message without taking away its spontaneity, its essential passion and life (ibid.: 112).

THE ARRANGEMENT AS STYLE

Taking into consideration the discussion above, an integral point that has been identified about Gerald Wilson's musical style is his arranging, orchestration, harmonic density, instrumental coloring, and the wide range and diversity of his use of different instruments in different voicings. Ted Gioia sums up this concept in excellent fashion by noting that "Wilson's writing leans toward thick, textured sounds in which the arrangements are as prominent as the soloists" (Gioia 142).

Early Repertoire

One of the major ideals expressed by Wilson in his stylistic development has been his notion of harmonic extension. In addition, he enhanced this concept with a stylistic use of dense chord voicings. He has pointed out that even in his early arrangements and compositions for the Jimmie Lunceford Orchestra, he was attempting to use wider ranges and extended chordal structures. Attesting to this are the following observations of Alyn Shipton (2001):

> Another equally novel Wilson composition and arrangement for Lunceford, "Yard Dog Mazurka," was to become the basis of Stan Kenton's "Intermission Riff" . . . Lunceford's band was technically equipped to lay almost anything put in front of it, and, just as Gillespie had Calloways's band work its way through the advanced voicings of "Paradiddle" and "Pickin' the Cabbage," Wilson had Lunceford's orchestra trying out several of his equally advanced harmonic ideas. (515)

"Intermission Riff," the stepchild of "Yard Dog Mazurka," with the principal theme as taken by the Kenton orchestra, became one of that outfit's signature arrangements. As Wilson mentioned in chapter 3, the harmonic progressions he wrote for both "Hi Spook" and "Yard Dog Mazurka" had never been used in jazz. In the score section below, the principal harmonic scheme and melodic theme for "Yard Dog Mazurka" transpires measures 5–24.

In a sense, during his Lunceford years of 1939 to 1942, Wilson was forging some pre-bop concepts into his arrangements, and his eventual associations with Dizzy Gillespie and other modern musicians of the 1940s would provide more inspiration and stylistic interaction. Shipton (2001) notes that after Wilson left Lunceford's band while on tour to California in 1942, he eventually formed his own band and

> took his new line-up both into the Plantation and the Downbeat on Central Avenue. His musicians included the trombonist Melba Liston, whose early arrangements for the group show much of the secure grasp of modern jazz arranging she was later to display as a member of Dizzy Gillespie's 1950s orchestras.
>
> So, at the same time that Teddy Edwards and Howard McGhee were playing small-group bebop on the Avenue, well ahead of Parker and Gillespie's arrival, Wilson was playing big-band jazz which was developing many of the advanced harmonic ideas he had tried out with Lunceford. (516)

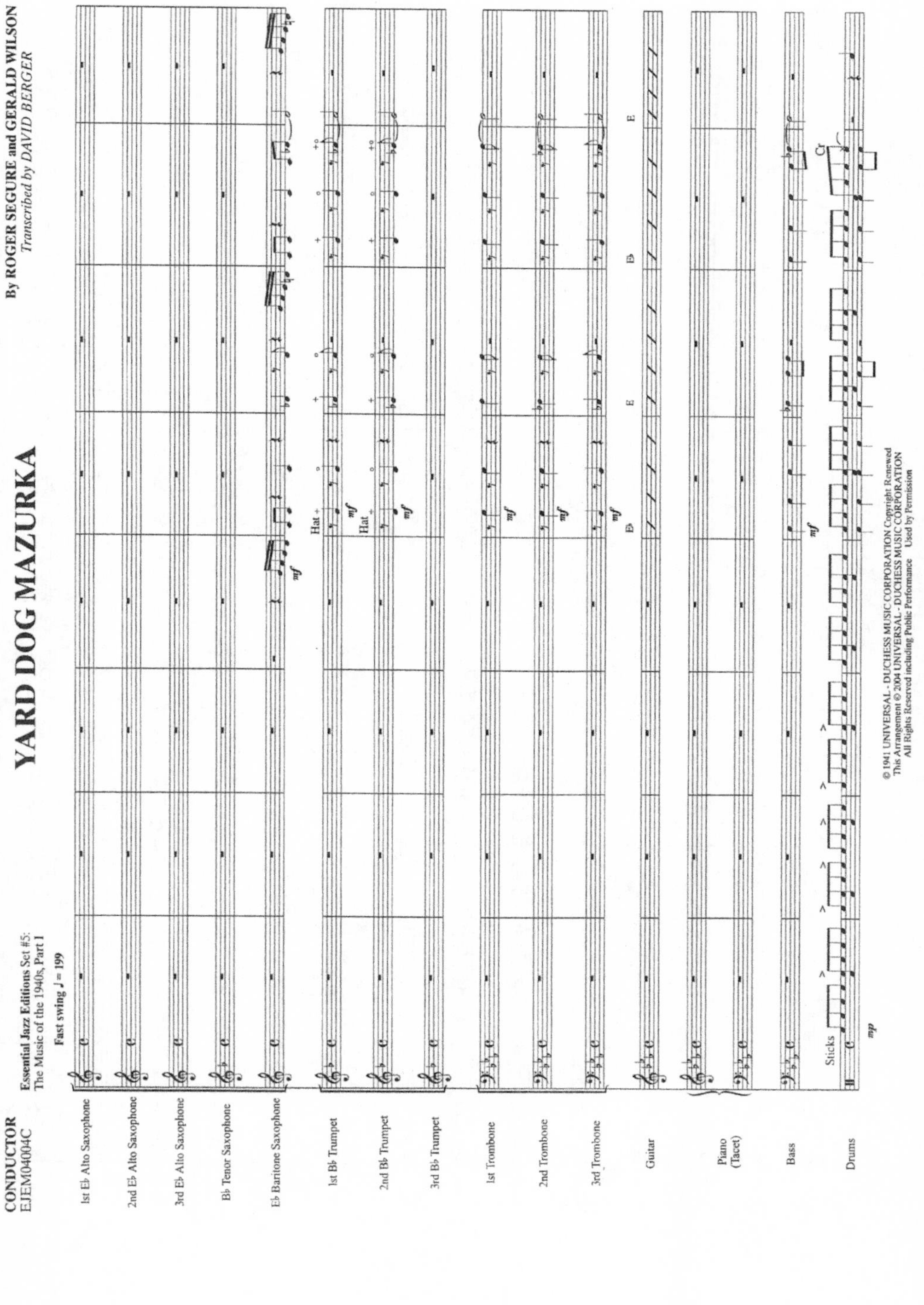

CONDUCTOR
EJEM04004C
Essential Jazz Editions Set #5:
The Music of the 1940s, Part I
YARD DOG MAZURKA
By ROGER SEGURE and GERALD WILSON
Transcribed by DAVID BERGER
Fast swing ♩ = 199
1st E♭ Alto Saxophone
2nd E♭ Alto Saxophone
3rd E♭ Alto Saxophone
B♭ Tenor Saxophone
E♭ Baritone Saxophone
1st B♭ Trumpet
2nd B♭ Trumpet
3rd B♭ Trumpet
1st Trombone
2nd Trombone
3rd Trombone
Guitar
Piano
(Tacet)
Bass
Drums
Sticks
Hat
Cr
© 1941 UNIVERSAL - DUCHESS MUSIC CORPORATION Copyright Renewed
This Arrangement © 2004 UNIVERSAL - DUCHESS MUSIC CORPORATION
All Rights Reserved including Public Performance Used by Permission

Yard Dog Mazurka

Conductor - 2

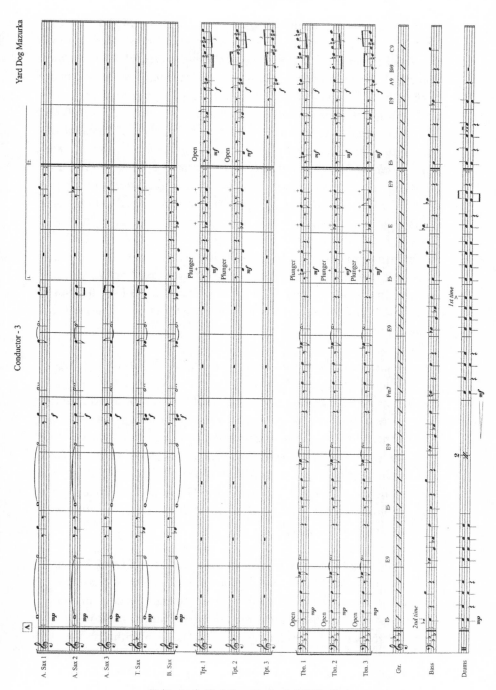

"Yard Dog Mazurka." Used with permission from the Gerald Wilson Estate.

Shipton also notes that discographer Chris Sheridan, in assessing the Armed Forces Radio Service (AFRS) "Jubilee" radio show broadcasts from Los Angeles,[3] concludes that the "boppish" band of Gerald Wilson is "more thoroughly modern—despite the swing-styled rhythm section—than any of the others" (Sheridan 1992/2006) on the AFRS recording. These "others" included the bands of Benny Carter, Wilbert Baranco, and Jimmy Mundy. Sheridan, like Shipton, a critic based in the United Kingdom, also makes an additional insightful observation in his liner notes, asserting that Gerald Wilson "has remained a leader of vigorous but underrated orchestras to this day" (1992/2006). In his final assessment of the 1946 AFRS recordings of Wilson, Carter, Baranco, and Mundy, Sheridan makes the following conclusions:

> This was altogether a vibrant part of the end of an era. But jazz always manages to have its tomorrows and Los Angeles would come in the next decade with a Californian brand of small group jazz built directly on the ensemble and rhythmic principles of the Swing Era heard here. (ibid.)

Of great interest is the above observation that Gerald Wilson was surpassing his contemporary bandleaders in terms of "modernism," and this can be directly linked to the point addressed earlier that he was incorporating progressive harmonic concepts before much of the bebop movement had penetrated the big-band style of others. A prime example of this is Wilson's arrangement of Dizzy Gillespie's "Groovin' High," recorded by the Gerald Wilson Orchestra in Los Angeles in 1945. It was the first big-band arrangement of the piece, and was recorded before Gillespie had even formed his own big band. Shipton (2001) makes note of the progressive nature of the arrangement and its recording:

> On Wilson's 1945 disc of "Groovin' High," Hobart Dotson's high-note trumpet and Eddie Davis's tenor solos are an uneasy compromise between the rapidity of bebop and the clichés of swing, but the ensemble writing is consistently adventurous. . . . Wilson's 1945 and early 1946 discs, including a riotous "Cruisin' with Cab," show

---

3. Shipton mistakenly cites New York as the broadcasting site for the AFRS recordings, whereas Los Angeles was the actual production location. See Sheridan (1992/2006).

that bebop was being played in large-band form within months of Parker and Gillespie's sextet discs, and well before Gillespie's own orchestra started to record. (516)

Shipton cites the fact that Wilson made a significant point during his interview with him (ibid.: 517), specifically paraphrasing that

big-band bebop was entirely different from small-group improvisation, because the arranger was predetermining harmonies that an improvising soloist was likely only to alight upon in passing. . . . It underlines, I believe, why the big-band format held such a continual fascination for Dizzy Gillespie. (517–18)

Upon listening to the 1945 recording of "Groovin' High," recorded in Los Angeles on the Excelsior label by the first Gerald Wilson Orchestra, one can hear a clear example of how Wilson was even reconstructing bop harmonic practices. It was also the first big-band arrangement of the tune. As Wilson pointed out in chapter 3, by 1945 he was already extensively using alternate chords—e.g., in place of a B flat minor chord, he would use the alternate of D flat major. Wilson also noted that he had already introduced the augmented eleventh in the thirteenth chord and that other bands were not using the voicing at that time.

"Hard Bop"

Mark C. Gridley (2003: 199) has expressed his view that "during the late 1950s and through the 1960s, several big bands drew from the sound of hard bop. The three most prominent were led by trumpeters Maynard Ferguson (1928–2006), Gerald Wilson (1918–2014), and Thad Jones (1923–1986)," the latter co-directed by drummer Mel Lewis, who had also played with Wilson's orchestra. Gridley makes an interesting comparison of Wilson's and Jones's bands, noting that they both used local all-star jazz musicians from, respectively, Los Angeles and New York, and did not conduct major tours, performing mostly in their own cities. He notes that "Wilson employed some of the best bop-style musicians to be found outside of New York, several of whom had become known to jazz fans long before they recorded with him" (ibid.: 200). Gridley also made the point that

Wilson molded a unique new sound from several sources. He used outstanding hard bop soloists who played with the ferocity and bluesy mood which jazz fans had come to expect from the combos of Art Blakey, Horace Silver, and Cannonball Adderley. He used an original arranging style. . . . It was hard and relentless. Each piece created and sustained a consistent mood. . . . By comparison with all other big bands, the Wilson band achieved a groove that more closely resembled hard bop. (ibid.: 201)

Thus, Gridley's impression of Wilson's style is one of hard bop. While this is an agreeable perspective, it can be argued that Wilson was hard bop yet saturated with a mixture of added and multiple flavors—e.g., his use of rhythms not employed in either "hard" nor "cool" bop, such as the Spanish/Mexican paso doble *adapted in "Carlos" and other similar pieces, the Cuban* cha cha chá *feel of "Viva Tirado," or the Cuban/Mexican* bolero *genre and origin of "La Mentira." In rhythmic and harmonic aspects, these styles are not part of the so-called "hard bop" style. Melodically, yes, the instrumentalists will play bop-styled improvisation, phrasing, and other expressive interpretation, but all of this cannot be reduced to the concept of hard bop. A large part of the issue I have with Gridley's assessment is that of terminology. Gerald Wilson's band, as well as those of Thad Jones, Mel Lewis, and Maynard Ferguson, at times performed styles that transcended descriptions such as hard bop, cool bop, traditional, modern, or progressive.*

Finally, Gridley cites Wilson's pieces "Moment of Truth" and "Viva Tirado" as originals "that had the raw ferocity of hard bop as well as a certain exoticism" (ibid.: 201). Again, I am not sure I can agree with Gridley's stylistic interpretation, as his descriptive terms are, to me, overly categorical. Gerald Wilson's style often transcends such labeling.

One final point: Gridley was also quoted above as assessing the Ferguson/Jones/Wilson triad as leading the three most prominent big bands drawing from the hard bop sound during the late 1950s through the 1960s. I would respond to this by citing the emergence of a number of other prominent big bands during the same period that also evoked considerable hard bop styles, e.g., the bands of Buddy Rich, Oliver Nelson, and Eddie "Lockjaw" Davis (although not highly promoted, an outstanding group), not to mention previous bop-oriented bands that continued into the 1960s, including those of Woody Herman and Lionel Hampton, among others.

"Blues for Yna Yna." Used with permission from the Gerald Wilson Estate.

A mid-career example of Wilson's steadfast innovation in traditional jazz forms is his "Blues for Yna Yna," recorded on his first Pacific Jazz LP, You Better Believe It (1961). A minor blues piece constructed on a medium-tempo, 3/4 jazz waltz meter, the main theme is a dynamic interplay of brass, saxophones, and flute. Based on a twenty-four-bar blues framework, the flavor takes some unconventional twists at the IV and V chord sections at measures 9 and 17 (see above), incorporating altered and extended chords. In 1961, Wilson was taking a very unique and innovative approach to the minor blues in terms of rhythm, harmony, melody, and counterpoint.

Latin Works

"Viva Tirado," Wilson's most traveled and recorded composition, is one of many themes dedicated to specific bullfighters in addition to being among numerous pieces that can be placed in his Latin-inspired repertoire. But we must keep in mind that the Latin influence permeates much of his music in general, and as noted previously, jazz in general.

"Viva Tirado" is basically a cha cha chá, the Cuban form and rhythm that emerged during the fifties and sixties as a highly popular dance and period style, although it continues to be adapted in various Latin American, salsa, and Latin jazz contexts. Classically based on the 3–2 clave ♩ ♪ ♩ ♪ | 𝄾 ♩ ♩ 𝄾 it can also be constructed on the 2–3 clave depending on the arrangement; the latter "reverse" 𝄾 ♩ ♩ 𝄾 | ♩ ♪ ♩ ♪ clave can be adapted to "Viva Tirado."

Wilson related to me that he purposely based the principal motif of ♫ ♩ on the three syllables of "cha cha cha" as the theme's three opening *notes. Using the piano part below as a reference, "Viva Tirado" opens with a four-bar introduction on piano, bass, drums, and congas accenting the central rhythmic/harmonic timeline of the piece. Initiating the tune's basic AABA form, the trombone section, scored into the theme, enters at A. The saxophone section, built over the central motif, enters at $A_{(2)}$ in a unison, sustained note melodic theme, continuing in a similar although harmonically changing manner at B, or bridge section. It is in this bridge that Wilson makes use of some of his dense harmonic constructs, such as $D^b7^{(\#9)}$, $B^{bm}7^{(b5)}$, and $E^{b7(b9\#5)}$ chords. At C, the AABA head of the piece closes out with rhythm section, trombones, and saxophones repeating the $A_{(2)}$ orchestration.*

"Viva Tirado." Used with permission from the Gerald Wilson Estate.

Of interest as examples of Wilson's unique harmonic approach are the dense chordal figures in the trumpet solo background parts at measures 65–80 (see below). Wilson orchestrated these figures using the piano and the saxophone section, with trombone counterparts underneath.

Piano

Piano excerpt, "Viva Tirado." Used with permission from the Gerald Wilson Estate.

In 1971, trumpeter Freddie Hubbard recorded one of his original compositions, "First Light," which became the title track of his most widely known and highest-selling LP, earning a Grammy Award in 1972. One can easily note that Hubbard follows Wilson's thematic, harmonic, and rhythmic formula in "Viva Tirado," from the similar opening cha cha chá semiotic pattern to the bridge structure to the complete AABA format. Hubbard's recording is one of many illustrating the musical impact of the tune.

Wilson's 1966 recording of "Carlos" on his LP The Golden Sword *is another classic example of the composer's concept of the Latin dimension. It is based on one of Wilson's favorite musical intonations, that of the paso doble form often associated with the bullfight ambience of Spain, Mexico, and other Latin American countries. As notated in the opening measures of the piece below, Wilson applies the subtle and basic harmonic form deriving from the traditional paso doble, although with some harmonic extension, along with the use of the Cuban habanera rhythmic pattern in the bass (and baritone saxophone).*

PIANO/GUITAR

Piano/guitar excerpt, "Carlos." Used with permission from the Gerald Wilson Estate.

"Carlos" features a trumpet soloist, and the original musician Wilson selected for this seminal recording was Jimmy Owens, a New York City native who has led his own groups in addition to performing with Lionel Hampton, Charles Mingus, Dizzy Gillespie, and Count Basie, among many others. In his interpretation of the solo part on "Carlos," Owens achieves the portrait and emotiveness that Wilson wanted in his tone poem for the matador Carlos Arruza. Owens works the main theme (see below) in an evocative opening statement, reiterates it as the tune *modulates from the C tonic to the F subdominant mode, and proceeds to create some inspiring improvisation of the theme. Wilson constantly reinforces the arrangement with piercing yet subtle melodic/rhythmic phrases in the parts for the reeds and brass, consistently developing and evoking the spirit of the paso doble and the bull ring.*

SOLO TRUMPET

CARLOS

Dedicated to Carlos Arruza
and Fine Trumpet Players

COMPOSED AND ARRANGED BY
GERALD WILSON

Solo trumpet part, "Carlos." Used with permission from the Gerald Wilson Estate. Continued on following page.

Solo trumpet part, "Carlos." Used with permission from the Gerald Wilson Estate.

I must also add some very subjective words here concerning this piece. Through his performance of "Carlos," Jimmy Owens, in his role as trumpet soloist, evokes the spirit and soul of many meanings of the piece. As I listen, the words subtle strength, bravery, risk, contrition, *and* love *come to my mind. I soak in his rich and loving tone. He tells us how important this piece is, and how honored he is to be the one playing it. He is the matador.*

The work done by Wilson on his Detroit *album, the bulk of which was recorded in 2009, deserves some attention in this chapter, which is dedicated to a small fraction of his full oeuvre. Specifically, we should focus on the fifth movement of the* Detroit *suite, "Before Motown." In the movement, Wilson recalls the period before Detroit's innovative move into popular music that became known as "Motown," perhaps best translated as black popular music of the "Motor City," Detroit, and spearheaded by producer Berry Gordy and his entourage of artists recording on his Motown Records label. Wilson chooses to adapt the same Latin* cha cha *concept that he had used on his 1962 composition of "Viva Tirado." Using the same two-bar rhythmic vamp as the central motif, he proceeds to construct an overlaying melodic theme projected by the saxophone and trumpet sections (see measures 9–40 in score below), also similar to the "Viva Tirado" saxophone head.*

"Before Motown" (measures 1–40). Used with permission from the Gerald Wilson Estate.

"Before Motown" (measures 1–40). Used with permission from the Gerald Wilson Estate.

""Before Motown"• Score • pg. 4 of 29

"Before Motown" (measures 1–40). Used with permission from the Gerald Wilson Estate.

"Before Motown" (measures 1–40). Used with permission from the Gerald Wilson Estate.

"Before Motown" (measures 1–40). Used with permission from the Gerald Wilson Estate.

"Before Motown" (measures 1–40). Used with permission from the Gerald Wilson Estate.

"Before Motown" (measures 1–40). Used with permission from the Gerald Wilson Estate.

"Before Motown" (measures 1–40). Used with permission from the Gerald Wilson Estate.

"Before Motown" (measures 1–40). Used with permission from the Gerald Wilson Estate.

"Before Motown" (measures 1–40). Used with permission from the Gerald Wilson Estate.

At section B, the harmonic progression of the piece continues to follow a I-ᵇII-ᵇIII two-measure structure, changing to a ten-bar framework and modulating to V — ᵇVI — ᵇVII for another ten bars, returning to the ten-bar I — ᵇII — ᵇIII construct (see measures 1/11–42 below). This feel or form is what I would loosely refer to as a "flamenco blues." Of interest is that phrases are based on ten-bar instead of eight-bar frameworks, which to most might be the norm. Thus, the cyclic form comprises thirty bars instead of the more common twenty-four that would often encompass a melodic head in addition to chorus sections for improvisation. Wilson basically constructs the piece on a Spanish paso doble rhythm sitting on a Cuban cha cha chá concept. At the outset, the bass invokes a basic Cuban habanera pattern (♩. ♪♩ ♩) adhering to a 2–3 clave. But this music also evokes the spirit and style of specific contemporary jazz artists active during the 1960s, including Miles Davis, John Coltrane, and Lee Morgan, who used various interpretive frameworks similar to the harmonic concept used here—e.g., Davis's LP Sketches of Spain, Morgan's "The Gigolo," and assorted Coltrane recordings, all evocative of a certain Spanish hue. The question can arise as to who was the first to use this formula—Wilson or the latter artists? Or does it really matter? Jelly Roll Morton referred to the "Spanish tinge" in jazz in 1938 (Lomax 1938). Duke Ellington composed "Caravan" with Puerto Rican trombonist Juan Tizol in 1936, and Dizzy Gillespie wrote "Manteca" with the Afro-Cuban conguero Chano Pozo in 1947.

*   Chick Corea used Spanish and African inspirations in vast quantities. "Before Motown" evokes the soul of these artists and so many more. But the approach of Gerald Wilson remains unique. Unlike much or most of the Latin influence in jazz, based on Afro-Cuban genres, most of Wilson's inspiration for the Latin element derives from Mexican or Spanish forms (although "Before Motown," "Viva Tirado," and other compositions do tap into the Cuban base).*

""Before Motown"• Score • pg. 12 of 29

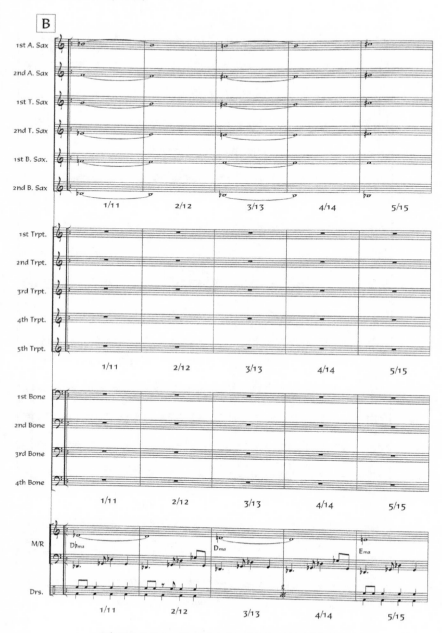

"Before Motown" (measures 11–42). Used with permission from the Gerald Wilson Estate.

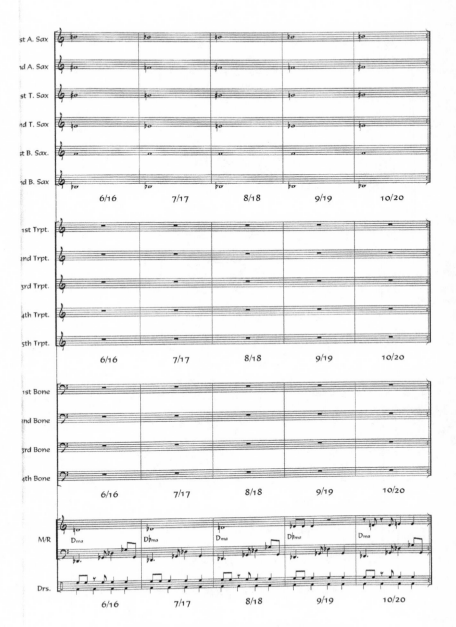

"Before Motown" (measures 11–42). Used with permission from the Gerald Wilson Estate.

""Before Motown"• Score • pg. 14 of 29

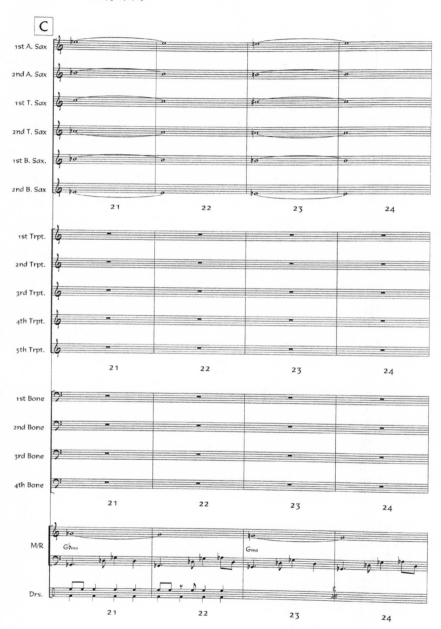

"Before Motown" (measures 11–42). Used with permission from the Gerald Wilson Estate.

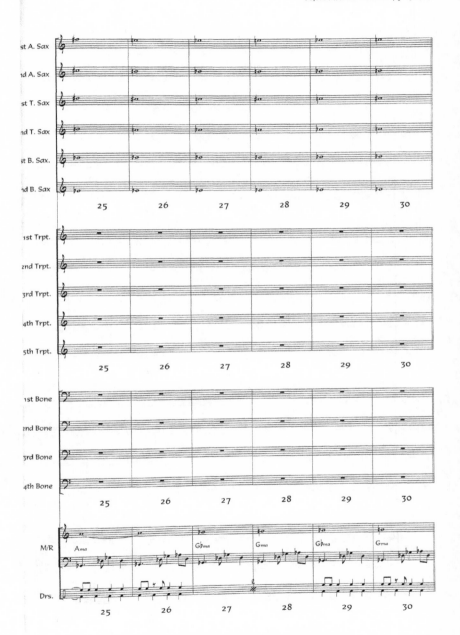

"Before Motown" (measures 11–42). Used with permission from the Gerald Wilson Estate.

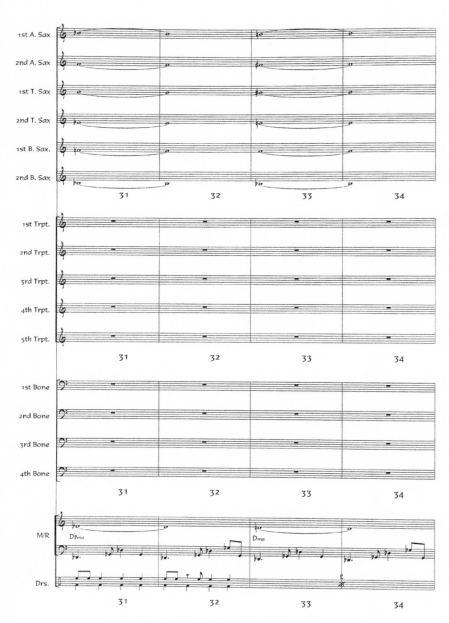

"Before Motown" (measures 11–42). Used with permission from the Gerald Wilson Estate.

"Before Motown" (measures 11–42). Used with permission from the Gerald Wilson Estate.

"Before Motown" (measures 11–42). Used with permission from the Gerald Wilson Estate.

"Before Motown" features dynamic improvised solos from Wilson's Los An-geles orchestra. Trumpeter Bobby Rodríguez, a native of east Los Angeles, takes the initial improvisation role after the introductory themes, and one of the tenor saxophonists follows. Simultaneous trombone and trumpet solos are offered by Erik Jorgenson and Sean Jones, and another intricate yet tasty piano solo caps the improvisations, with Brian O'Rourke display-ing a style highly reminiscent of another West Coast jazz pianist, Vince Guaraldi. The arrangement thus features a rich diversity of orchestration and soloists representing an intersecting and wide stylistic range. Of sig-nificant, even symbolic, musical interest is the final section (section F; see below) that closes the arrangement, a twenty-four-measure "coda" of sorts that personifies the extended chord structure that has highlighted Wilson's style throughout his career, although in a consistently evolving framework (giving the section a "Hard Latin" written direction at the outset). Wilson develops the motif of the movement with dense harmonic movement.

"Before Motown"• Score • pg. 24 of 29

"Before Motown" (final section). Used with permission from the Gerald Wilson Estate.

""Before Motown"• Score • pg. 26 of 29

"Before Motown" (final section). Used with permission from the Gerald Wilson Estate.

From a Musical Point of View: Musical Philosophy and Style

"Before Motown" (final section). Used with permission from the Gerald Wilson Estate.

"Before Motown" • Score • pg. 28 of 29

"Before Motown" (final section). Used with permission from the Gerald Wilson Estate.

PROGRESSIVE INNOVATIONS

"Triple Chase" is an up-tempo, progressive hard bop tune composed by Wilson and originally recorded in 1981 on his Lomelin *album. He renamed the piece "Sax Chase" for the 2005 CD,* In My Time. *The arrangement features three tenor saxophonists improvising sequential solos through a complex set of chord changes, incorporating diverse altered and extended chords. Below are the first solo section chord changes with the basic orchestral background figurations, in Wilson's own hand, of the arrangement.*

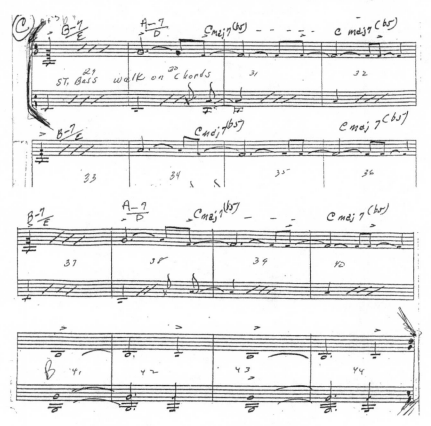

Chord changes, "Triple Chase." Used with permission from the Gerald Wilson Estate.

The five-part suite Theme for Monterey, *commissioned for the 1997 Monterey Jazz Festival and released as a CD in 1998 on the MAMA foundation label (see Chapter 6), is a prime example of how Wilson's composition and orchestration style continued to evolve. The principal theme and harmonic structure of the suite (see master rhythm and soprano saxophone charts below) is heard throughout all five movements, taking various forms of development, rhythmic metamorphosis, and improvisation. The subtle, lush opening eight bars of the first movement, titled "Romance," are highlighted by pensive, falling piano octaves over sustained ensemble orchestrations characteristic of Wilson's signature thick, densely voiced chordal mixes, attaining a slowly building and mild crescendo, at which*

"Theme for Monterey" (master rhythm). Used with permission from the Gerald Wilson Estate.

point soprano saxophone enters with the master theme of the suite. Scott Mayo delivers a free interpretation of the melody with creative embellishments at strategic spaces. Of interest in the arrangement is Wilson's written chord notation for piano in addition to chord symbols. The first movement effect of the forty-bar melodic/harmonic theme draws us into a richly thought-out and conceptualized tone portrait of Wilson's favorite sites in Monterey. The recorded suite stands high among the composer's long list of recorded work.

SOPRANO SAX

"Theme for Monterey" (soprano saxophone). Used with permission from the Gerald Wilson Estate.

THE DIMINISHED TRIANGLE AND EIGHT-PART HARMONY

As reflected in many of Wilson's compositions and arrangements, and alluded to in chapter 6, much of his compositional style and orchestration has largely been characterized by what he has referred to as the diminished triangle and eight-part harmony. He explained these concepts as follows:

Wilson: The diminished triangle . . . there are three diminished [seventh] chords, and three times four [notes in each chord] are twelve, and so they take in the whole twelve notes that we have. We only have twelve notes and there are only three diminished [seventh chords]. And this opens up not only to people that are writing music, but say for instance, great improvisers. Once they learn the secret of the three diminished [seventh] chords, they have already learned the whole scope of what we have in music today as far as tones are concerned. That means that they are never in trouble when they are improvising because it's always there. No matter what your chord is. And the guys who have learned this, they are great improvisers. They don't have to struggle, "Oh this is F7, this is sharp 9", or whatever. This of course doesn't matter to him. . . . Of course, in the process of all of this your ear is training itself. You know your ear is training itself. And you're beginning to hear all of this. I mean, they don't care what you play. They are home. . . . Take your three notes. Take C, D, and E. C dim. 7, D dim. 7, and E dim. 7. And you've covered all twelve [notes]. You've covered all twelve of them. They're right there.

As clarified in the schematic below, the three diminished seventh, four-note chords on C, D, and E envelop all twelve notes of the chromatic scale.

C D♯ F♯ A

D F G♯ B

E G A♯ C♯

Wilson has adapted his concept of the diminished triangle through the years, and one of his most recent recordings In My Time *(2005), briefly*

profiled in chapter 6, includes a three-part suite, The Diminished Triangle, *directly constructed on the technique in addition to utilizing his
eight part harmony orchestration.*

Wilson: [With] the players today, of course, there's a different thing going
in jazz and that's why the bands of yesterday, the bands of the fifties and the
sixties and the seventies and up to now, that's why they all sound alike. First
of all, they're always playing four-part harmony. Secondly, they're trying
to fool you with a lot of different lines coming from here and there. Which
is really getting in the way. In jazz, improvisation is so important. When
the solos are playing, I've noticed these arrangers have the saxophone
running all along the background. Here's a guy trying to create. Because
improvisation is creativity. He's trying to create. He's [the arranger] got
the saxophone running all over the place, the trombone running all over
the place. You know, jazz, you can't clutter it up with a lot of notes. You
can't clutter it up with a lot of notes because then you hinder the feeling
that is necessary to play jazz. You've got to have a certain feeling to play
jazz anyway. And that is why the new style that's out now has all been
befuddled. How are we going to play [on top of that style] like Wynton
Marsalis and Roy Hargrove and Terence Blanchard? If you're in jazz now,
first you got to—as a writer and as a player too—to be able to hear, take
for instance, the sharp 9. They don't really realize the importance of the
sharp 9. Because the sharp 9 is actually the sound of the blues and what it
gives you is, it gives you the major and minor simultaneously. You know?
So, in the old days, they have their blue notes. Well, the blue note in the
key of C would be the sharp 9. What happens is, the sharp 9, which is what
they call the blue note, they would make it like a minor chord. Because
they wouldn't play that major third. They wouldn't play that major third
in there. You understand? For instance, "D flat 7" is the sharp 9 and that's
necessary in jazz to give you the feeling of jazz, because jazz was out of
the blues, it's not jazz. You gotta play the blues. You can play the blues in
everything. You play the blues in Rimsky-Korsakov's *Hymn to the Sun.*
You can play the blues in church. You can play the blues everywhere. It's
the folk music. It's the folk music of black people and they've gotta realize
that this is what's happening with blacks. It's their folk music.
Loza: It's not like you can learn it from some purely mechanical, unspiritual basis.

Wilson: I hear a guy playing, if I've heard him three nights in a row, I've heard his whole repertoire unless he is a sincere, dedicated jazz musician that's continually searching for jazz. You continue. Your search never ends in jazz. But I can hear you, you can learn this exercise backwards and forwards and every kind of way. But you don't have the other necessary thing to pull it off. You have your little repertoire that you've built up and that's it. Whereas the guy that's continually searching, that's why you notice . . . they make it their business to start somewhere else all the time. Last night he started here. Tonight he's not going to start and play that same thing again. Now you have guys that do that. They play the same solo every night in each number that they play. They play the same solo. The guys are searching for jazz. We got a lot of them. We've got these young kids, they're into new things. You know, jazz is a thing that's continually moving. It's a chain of evolution, each little link. . . . In other words, we can't have the most modern that we have today and not have ragtime. Do you understand? We can't have one without the other. It all came in the time. When it wears out. . . . It doesn't wear out; it just takes its place.

Loza: Have you encountered, then, in your band through the years, musicians who come in with this technical, polished, mechanical [approach], but unspiritual? . . . Because that's what you're talking about. The dedication beyond the materialist thing of just the notes and the structure. Have you had musicians who come in, who in spite of being an incredible virtuoso, cannot adapt to what you're talking about and they're just playing a bunch of mechanical notes and it doesn't work?

Wilson: Absolutely, it doesn't work. . . . I've had them in my band. But it took me a while to realize that hey, I've heard your whole repertoire. I know exactly what you're gonna play. Whereas, I get a man here like Harold Land. Harold Land. He's a jazz man. And he played with some of the greatest that there were to play with. He could play with any of them. And he had the feeling of it. And he made transitions. He didn't just play like he always played. At one time, I heard Harold Land . . . I thought he was a blues saxophone player, but he can play the blues, which is another thing that all guys must realize that you're gonna have to play the blues if you're gonna play jazz.

Loza: You know, it's like music is a prayer in many ways and if you're just gonna recite the prayer without thinking about it, you're not feeling it. It's gonna be the same litany. But if you say it, if you're saying it different every time, then that means you're thinking, if you're taking it very seriously. But you really believe, you're not just rattling. . . . So this dimension of the spiritual in jazz is very important, I think, to all of us, and you're talking about it because there seems to be a belief in the philosophy and the teaching of jazz today . . . that's got nothing to do with jazz. Jazz is just. . . . You gotta learn it technically and play it. And then again, you end up with this dry, empty product. Yeah, the guy sounds just like John Coltrane but that's the problem. He sounds just like Sonny Rollins. That's the problem. We get students that come and do auditions here and they want to read a solo out of one of these transcribed Charlie Parker books and we say you can't do that. That's not jazz. But they think they can. So something is wrong, I guess, and could it be that it's [due to] that lack of the spontaneous and of the spiritual that students are being told that you can learn jazz from this book? There's nothing wrong with a book, but can you really learn jazz from just a book and recordings?

Wilson: I don't think so. You can learn to do something, not be a dedicated jazz musician, because you're not going to be in jazz long anyway unless you're really tough. You're going to have to be really putting something out there. Because jazz is going to weed you out anyway. It's gonna weed you out. If you are mediocre it's gonna weed you out. Now we know that there are those that can get along with being mediocre. I think it was even last year when they presented. I gotta get the exact words that he said. I didn't hear them myself, but they're presenting an award to Oscar Peterson. This was at the IAJE [International Association of Jazz Education]. And he explained to them that they were teaching mediocrity. They're teaching mediocrity. This is what you're teaching now. You're not teaching . . . well, of course what else are you going to teach if you take a look at, where's your teacher, what did he do? Did he play jazz? Was he in jazz? Or did he just read a book? And he says, "Well, I can teach the history 'cause I know this is the history. I can read the history books and I'll know about the history!" You know? No, that's good, but if you run across a guy that was there during the history of it, he knows much more about it than what you read in this book. Because books can be written as to what you want them to say.

During one of the interviews, Wilson also reflected in some detail on his concept of eight-part harmony.

Wilson: I feel that this link that I have will enable them to get more harmony than four parts. Most arrangers today are still using four-part harmony, doubling, doubling the lead with the sax section with five. Of course, I give them five notes every now and then. I devised a way to get five different notes all of the time. In other words, that can also happen, which I exhibited in "Anthropology." My recording on "Anthropology." The actual theme of anthropology is harmonized in five parts and that's never been done before. So you have to know what to do to do that. . . . In other words, you won't have to just double. And, of course, the ensemble things, which are very big in jazz now, orchestral jazz we're talking about, the things will open up a way for them to do more harmony. In other words, why have eight brass if they're all going to play the same four notes. You have four trumpets and they're going to play, and then the trombones are going to play the same notes. And then the reed section, four of them are going to play the same notes. Then you're going to double the baritone and maybe every now and then he falls in on a fifth part. Well, this will open up the door for writers to be able to do this. It's highly technical. It's no trick because when you write it, all you gotta do is know what your chord is, your bass note is telling you the name of the chord. It's telling you the name of the chord. Plus, you have the advantage now of playing major/minor simultaneously. During all of this, you are using flat 9, sharp 9, and augmented 11ths and 13ths and you're getting eight different notes on the chord. That does not take away. It's not a trick. It actually should be there. All of this is available to writers now and we're going to put it in the book for those who haven't discovered it yet. Those who may have seen a chord . . . I used to do it just to see . . . just to get a reaction. Years ago, I would just do it on one chord. Nobody was paying attention and then they said, "Oh yeah, that's a nice chord."

Loza: I remember when I first heard your recordings, like thirty years ago, that I would hear this extended harmony, and that's what drew me to it. And, of course, it was within the jazz thing, but nobody else was sounding like that . . . I think years later Thad Jones was sounding like that, but not at the time you were doing it. That's my impression. Even Ellington extended the chords, but I was hearing thirteenth chords with all kinds of flats. Of course, I think it goes beyond that, which is one other question that I wanted to ask. And we'll look at this when we look at your scores and actually look at the chord structure and the way and the kinds of chord symbols and structures you use; but when you're do-ing this eight-part harmony, is it the kind of harmony that you can call a thirteenth chord, an eleventh chord, or is it something that cannot be described like that?

Wilson: Oh no, it can be . . . because the way that I was able to protect it during the time when I was coming up [was] because I had many people I would seek on to look at my score, because I didn't have to put the whole thing down—all I had to do was put the head—all I had to do was give him the one that said flat 9 and that was the only one that I would give to him, just the flat 9, the F7 and the flat 9. But then over here I'm playing another chord, a completely different chord. You have the four notes up here. I don't tell you what's up there. I don't put it up there.

Loza: Exactly, you just write it in the parts, in the horn parts . . . so in other words, you had different chords being played.

Wilson: Yeah, it was a whole other chord. He's only playing the flat 9.

Loza: But the piano player was just playing the chords. And then you had another chord structure within the trumpet section. So there's really no way to explain it like all in one chord.

Wilson: No, not in one chord. See, you have to know how to work the puzzle. You know, there's a puzzle, they're just like zigzag, a jigsaw puzzle. There's this one little key here that, "Hey, there it is. It doesn't work here." It doesn't work here either. So you gotta know where it works. I've seen many, many . . . even Duke put it right out—but he didn't know how to work it on everything. But I say that so that I can document it. I've documented it many times. So you know where it came from. This thing about things coming out of the air and it just fell out of the heavens. It didn't just fall out of the heavens. And, of course, I studied very hard, a lot of classical music during that period when I disbanded my band, of course to be able to write for the symphony orchestra. And I studied the great composers. And there were things that I was able to get from them. But then I can think of even classical music, listening to so much of it; now all classical music isn't great either, you know? There's a thing in a Stravinsky thing. He's got this brass little thing, you know? It would have been wonderful and all he had to do was to use the diminished triad and he would have had this whole brass section playing eight different notes, and nine—and ten.

CHAPTER 9

CONCLUSION AND CONTINUATION
The Mestizaje *of Gerald Wilson*

My Lord calls me,
He calls me by the thunder,
The trumpet sounds it in my soul.
— NEGRO SORROW SONG
FROM W. E. B. DU BOIS, *THE SOULS OF BLACK FOLK*

During the writing of this chapter, I learned of Wilson's passing on September 8, 2014.

How does one decide to reflect or to make some sort of culminating assessment of Gerald Wilson, his life, and his music? I have a problem with the concept of "final," or "conclusion," because Wilson's spirit and art continue to live in the present as much as in the past or the future. In fact, it thrives indefinitely, and from my perspective, infinitely.

But I would like to express an idea about Wilson that comes from my own experience and from my own mode of study. Wilson is a mosaic. He comes from a very African American context, a place, a heritage—something that molded him and that he proceeded to mold into life. Wilson has never stood still. He was always seeking change and renewal, challenges and learning, innovative newness and tradition.

All of these spaces through time also represent an ever-rotating mosaic of colors, shapes, and culture, and the various cultures within that Wilson has known, crossed through, embraced, and transformed with creative energy, consistently evolving a unique aesthetic cognition that only his music can explain, and in a nonverbal way.

As noted before, this interstice of cultures and thought is conceptual-
ized in Latin America as mestizaje, *the mixing of race and culture. Wilson*
has mixed the blues, gospel, and Western classical music he was exposed
to during a Mississippi childhood and subsequent moves to Memphis,
Chicago, Detroit, New York, among a diversity of domestic and global
workings of his art. He found his way to a destination, Los Angeles, that
became his base, and perhaps even a symbol—but never a place to stop his
creative production, nor a place that he could not leave to work his craft
in so many other places with artists, students, and an always captivated
public.

Wilson has mixed the musical ideas of Stravinsky, Khachaturian,
and Debussy with modern jazz concepts; he has studied the techniques
of repertoire of symphonic composers and integrated approaches with his
own compositions; he has adapted Latin American and Spanish cultural/
musical sources, creating new forms similar to the new forms of life that
have emerged from his marriage to Josefina Villaseñor; and he has ex-
perimented with progressive jazz elements, while never abandoning the
essence and purpose of the blues.

In his book The Mestizo Mind, *Serge Gruzinski (2002) critiques the*
significance of Latin American culture as that of multiple identities—a
mosaic, so to speak, of ideas, thoughts, beliefs, and creative energy related
to the multiple cultures that have especially intertwined the cognition of
the Latin American. This way of thinking of how the mind absorbs culture
can be applied to many societies. But in Wilson's music, as with Latin
America, it happened quickly. Wilson intersected his culture with the
cultures he learned. Even his innovations of multiple harmonies reflect
mestizaje, *as he identified with multiple voicings as a way to achieve*
newness, of survival, of looking forward to adapt the undone, the foreign,
the other.

Related to the type of perspective I have presented above are both some
contemporary and classic writings. In his five-year study of jazz musicians
in Accra, Ghana, Steven Feld (2012) focuses on the idea of cosmopoli-
tanism, reflecting on the various aesthetic practices and international
interface in the music of Ghanaians Ghanaba (Guy Warren), Nii Otoo
Annan, and Nii Noi Nortey.

Ghanaba had searched for creative and spiritual meaning in African
musical culture, American jazz, and European classical music, among

other global expressions. His response to Feld's inquiry about his jazz cosmopolitanism was that "the cosmopolitan label implies an ability to be at ease in many places" (82). Ghanaba's experiences in America had been, in his words, not at ease during his earlier years, but perhaps more at ease in later years, as he eventually found himself.

Feld reminds us that his Accra stories may resonate with "well-known multicultural cosmopolitanisms, like the world of W. E. B. Du Bois's 'double consciousness'"—Du Bois, interestingly, left the US for Ghana in his later life, passing away in Accra—"or Homi Bhabba's 'in-betweenness' or of Trin T. Minh-ha's 'modes of dwelling' as the motion between two" (48). Feld adds two other points of insight to this matrix: Paul Gilroy's "multilocal belonging," describing the idea as the ground "Gilroy figures as a critical foundation to planetary humanism"; and reading his Accra stories "as reaching toward the cosmopolitanism of Kwame Anthony Appiah's concept of 'universalism plus difference'" (48–49).

In her book California Polyphony: Ethnic Voices, Musical Crossroads *(2008), Mina Yang critiques the "ideology of multiculturalism" with specific reference to the cultural context of California, noting that in spite of a history of interracial conflict, "with its origin in cosmopolitanism and its foreseeable future in an increasingly evident pluralism, California celebrates its diversity as a source of strength and pride" (3). But Yang also cites cultural critic Lisa Lowe, who cautions against naïve interpretations of multiculturalism. Yang thus notes that Lowe, in her essay "Imagining Los Angeles in the Production of Multiculturalism" (1996), describes two contrasting representations of Los Angeles—the dystopic picture of a future Los Angeles, a pastiche of the third world, which Ridley Scott conjured up in the 1982 film* Blade Runner, *and the more utopic vision of the city as a site of multicultural spectacle as orchestrated by the 1990 Los Angeles Festival of the Arts, not unlike the more recent LA Arts Open House. According to Lowe, the images and narratives of pluralism promulgated by the festival, as well as by the LA Arts Open House, depoliticize multiculturalism by commodifying and containing difference, erasing actual geographical separations and historical disruptions, creating the illusion of inclusion, and obscuring real economic and social disparities. In effect, the performance of multiculturalism, enacted regularly in the name of interethnic harmony, reinforces the status quo by functioning as an "exotic, colorful advertisement of Los Angeles" (Yang: 3–4).*

GETTING TO THE GUT OF IT ALL

In the paragraphs above, I have outlined some thoughts on mestizaje, *hybridity, intercultural conflict and interculturalism, "the Other," and cosmopolitanism. The art of Gerald Wilson can certainly be described as mestizo. And it can be called cosmopolitan. Such work of such artists is frequently, if not usually, that of intercultural spaces of interface, collaboration, influence, reaction, resistance, and consolidation or rejection that occurs among artists of what Robin D. Kelley (1999) has conceptualized as polyculturalism, or what we may also recollect as experiences of diverse enculturation. In 1970, Albert Murray, in his book* The Omni-Americans: New Perspectives on Black Experience and American Culture, *was developing some similar concepts.*

But in spite of Wilson's extraordinary musico-cultural breadth, there remains a dimension of his ideology that dominates the above labels and analytical concepts. And that is his primal identity as a black man. Wilson made the issue clear in response to my questions as to whether or not formal study of jazz is sterilizing the tradition, or if it is a problem that there are so few blacks in so many college jazz orchestras.

Wilson: Well, I think that first of all we must remember where jazz really came from. First of all, jazz came from the slaves, slaves of America. They spent 249 years in slavery, but when they played a European instrument they played it different. They had a different way of playing. There is no jazz that originated in Kenya or Ghana, South Africa, North Africa. . . . They're black; the color is still the same. But they are not like the blacks from America. These blacks that were in America were different after 249 years. They had learned to speak this language as best they could by just hearing what their masters . . . (shall we say, the slave owners) . . . they just went hearing what they would say. If they would say, "Well, that is a bottle of water." Well, they couldn't get it out first what that was, and they said "dat" D-A-T, "dem," so you'll laugh at the way they're trying to talk but they are trying to do the best they can. No one's teaching them, you must remember. And remember for 249 years they weren't taking them like some little babies that we're going to teach. They beat them with whips to make them work every day from sun up until sun down. But after a while as things got a little better, not much better . . . because at my age now of eighty-four, this means that I've seen a lot that happened because

I was born in 1918. The point I'm trying to get over is, if you go to Cuba, you hear some guys over there playing some jazz. But they can't play it like the ones over here. They don't have the same feeling. They speak Spanish. They speak the Spanish language. And they . . . didn't go through what these slaves went through here, 249 years . . . it's a different mix all together. And even after they were emancipated it went on business as usual for years, just up until the sixties. Up until the sixties!

Loza: Until the Civil Rights Act and then still now.

Wilson: And even now. They still go through this. They have to go through this thing here. . . . But like I say, this thing called jazz; it is still . . . you know, it's all of the styles, all of the styles of jazz. First we start with ragtime, that's the first one that they made. Ragtime, New Orleans style, Dixieland, Chicago style, swing, bebop. These are all styles that the blacks created. They created bebop. They created swing. They created New Orleans style, Dixieland. They created it all.

Loza: Does it ever bother you that the tradition has changed from being in a jazz club with people having drinks, a good time, to what somebody might call a sterile student recital room where this student is playing a jazz solo in front of a faculty jury? Does that bother you?

Wilson: It doesn't bother me, of course, but I'm sure it must bother a lot of musicians. Because how are you going to have a guy telling you what to play, especially if you're a great player. The thing about jazz is, OK . . . it proves that it's an art form. You don't have to know a note from this room. You don't have to have ever studied the piano. We got guys who play the piano that can't read a note and they're the best. I mean, they're the best and so . . .

Loza: And they hear it and they see it and they don't think about what the note's name is.

Wilson: It doesn't mean a thing, you know? It's their music.

Loza: I still love classical music. I still want to write for orchestra. There's nothing wrong with that, but when you try to bring jazz to this very formal aesthetic that I am talking about, it sometimes can upset what jazz is about. Because jazz is not such a neat structured efficient thing all the time. Charlie Parker, like they said, he used to make his mistakes into notes. He used to turn his mistakes into part of the music. People like Lee Morgan would make mistakes because he took it to the edge. What is a mistake? There's no such thing as a mistake in jazz.

Wilson: What's a mistake?

Loza: But if you go to this other aesthetic, they will sit there and say, "Well, you missed that chord change, that was wrong. You have a rough sound." Well, a lot of people in jazz have a very rough sound. It doesn't mean it's bad. So, see, it's a very different experience, aesthetic, standard. And I'm talking about more of the type of people that took jazz and made it into an educational industry also. They wrote all these high school jazz band charts with notated solos so the students could read the solo, which is totally against the idea of jazz. . . . You talked about making jazz into a very structured art form and then you would end up with a jazz band and nobody could improvise, but they're all reading the jazz chart. This is what I'm talking about, Gerald. Is that a problem to you?

Wilson: Well, as I say again, it's not a problem to me, because again, jazz is my heritage. I don't have to think about it any other way than that it's my heritage. . . . Like I say, we have guys that dabble into symphonic. You might see one black. You might see two. Possibly you might see three. But I doubt if you're going to see four in any orchestra. You can go to every symphony orchestra in the world. It's not the black's cup of tea. Now we've got some that dabble in it . . .

Loza: But you have a lot of whites in jazz. It's not the same equation. In fact, there were all kinds of bands that were just white jazz bands.

Wilson: Oh yeah! That's what they're gonna all be now anyway. There are no more black bands. There's no more black bands. Blacks have been, shall we say, very . . . they keep them out. They won't teach them. You go to try to get into the jazz band here. And because, say he can't read as well . . . so they say, "Well, we have to pass you by."

Loza: That's exactly what I'm talking about Gerald.

Wilson: I was at Northridge for thirteen years. And in thirteen years I didn't see four blacks in any band or one in any band. They had one black out of Northridge. And he's still there. He was very good.

Loza: So this difference of the very ordered thing versus the very loose thing that is also ordered in its own way . . . the difference there, it doesn't bother you?

Wilson: It doesn't bother me because I know that jazz is going to still go on. It's going to still be the music of the blacks of America. That's it. I don't care what you do now. Nothing's gonna change that. Nothing's gonna change that! I mean, they're showing you the way to go all the time. I mean, all you gotta do is look at your trumpets, look at your trombones.

Whatever you look at. They excel. They excel. I mean, Joshua Redman and all of these heavies, young players that are playing saxophone, Antonio Hart and Jessie Davis and you know they're here. They're here. I just finished an album in New York City with all the New York City musicians. And we made a whole album in two days. In two days, you know?

But Wilson is simultaneously emphatic in his philosophy of not responding to the issues of race and racism from a racist perspective, which would undermine his hopes for true integration and his own history of integrating not only his orchestras, but his worldview.

Wilson: In the history of jazz, I've always given the whites their due. I've always given their due. Where they come in on the scene. I know when they came in on the scene. We know the first whites that played jazz. And I always give them their due. So I don't have that problem with wanting to give another race its credit for what they can do. So I don't have that problem. If I feel that I'm racially prejudiced, then I'm no better than the ones that are doing it on their sides. Just like on their sides I feel like they are not all that way. If it was not for people that were white, there are many things that happened for blacks that would not have happened at all.

Much of what Wilson has to say about the African American tradition, especially as related to music, relates and resonates in a salient fashion with the ideas expressed by scholar Christopher Small in his now-classic book Music of the Common Tongue: Survival and Celebration in African American Music *(1987).*

The fact is that Afro-American culture as it has developed over the last five-hundred years is a strategy which has been evolved by a highly creative and socially sophisticated people, using remembered, and indeed consciously and carefully transmitted, African ways of thought and perception as well as whatever elements of European and Euro-American culture came to hand, in order to make life worth living in a situation that was at best difficult and at worst desperate. (461)

The Afro-American tradition is the major music of the west in the twentieth century, of far greater human significance than those remnants of the great European classical tradition that are to be heard today in the concert halls and opera houses of the industrial world, east and west. (4)

For me, it is this persistently anarchistic resistance to classification of both the musicians and their music that is one of the enduring delights of Afro-American music . . . this anarchistic delight, which is, I am sure, part of the profoundly pluralistic inheritance that black people carry around with them still, not as a set of beliefs but as a style of thinking, feeling, perceiving—and of playing, listening and dancing. (5)

There can be very few people living in industrial societies who do not owe something, whether they admit or even realize it or not, to the power of the African vision of the world. (1)

I found increasingly that the music of this tradition fulfilled in me not only an emotional but also an intellectual and a social need which European classical music, however much I loved and admired much of it, did not, and if I was honest, never had fulfilled. (3)

Small's testimony *that African American music enhanced and inspired his intellectual and social perceptions also resonates with many of the thoughts of Cornel West, who in 1989 wrote that*

evaluation is never an end in itself (to preserve some eternal canon or further a political cause), but rather an integral by-product of a profound understanding of an art object, of how its form and content produce the multiple effects they do and of the role it plays in shaping and being shaped by the world of ideas, political conflicts, cultural clashes and the personal turmoils of its author and audience. . . . in examining how significant art objects (those that are accorded stature in the articulated canon and those that are not) offer insights into the human condition in *specific* time and places, but also shape our view of the current cultural *crisis*, we will hear the silences and see through the blind spots that exist alongside those insights. Art criticism *is* art history, but much intellectual baggage must be shed if we are to have a criticism commensurate with the complexities and challenges of our epoch, if we are to make history as well as to mine it. (West 1989: 446)

Of further resonance with these thoughts of multiple realities and recogni-tion of both canons and non-canons is the joint perspective of West and bell hooks, who identify the specific necessity for black intellectuals to link their discourse and critique, but not confine them to, "indigenous institutional practices permeated by the kinetic orality and emotional physicality, the rhythmic syncopation, the protean improvisation and the religious, rhetorical and antiphonal elements of Afro-American life" (hooks and West 1999: 312).

Small, West, and hooks also resonate with Antonio Gramsci's (1971) con-ceptualization of the "organic intellectual," whereby the artist, whether a Gerald Wilson or a Bessie Smith (the latter as concepted by Angela Davis, 1999), contributes to the philosophical thoughts and social values and evolv-ing aesthetics of a changing, concurrent society. Such artists transcend even the "organic" label offered by Gramsci, and become the intuitive, superor-ganic communicator that Benedetto Croce (1952) placed above the mortal intellectual.

We must open up to the individuals and groups we study as they personify a method and theory that they *have conceptualized, in order to attempt to understand how and why they do what they do, be it Gerald Wilson or any other great artist. The title of this concluding (and* continuing*) chapter included the term* mestizaje, *which I have adapted previously in this book. In contemplating this idea of the mixing of race and culture, José Antonio Robles Cahero (2003) has suggested that our work as scholars, like that of mestizo cultures—e.g., as with the case of Gerald Wilson's musical oeuvre—should make use of the multiple realities and identities we experience, whether in the form of academic disciplines or cultural/artistic contact and influence. Our enculturations can serve us in a way that transcends and improves any hegemonic canon or delusions of preconceived and biased prestige.*

To conclude these thoughts, I have asked Jeri Wilson, one of Wilson's daughters, to put into words what she and Wilson's family (specifically, her sister Nancy Jo and nephew Eric Otis) would want to express about this rich aspect of Wilson's artistry and worldview, that of recognizing and incorporating everyone and everything into his work and life, professionally and personally.

Perhaps poetically, these three individuals, of African American, Mexi-can, and other heritages, mix, in the spirit of their father and grandfather, with the thoughts above of Small, a white man, Cornel West, a black man, and bell hooks, a black woman.

• • •

Our father, Gerald Wilson, often said, "I am first and foremost a jazz musician." He had a strong sense of pride in being African American. His view was that African Americans are the creators of jazz and its foundation. Proud of that heritage, he also acknowledged that he had been influenced by the classical masters such as Stravinsky, Ravel, and Khachaturian. His mother, Lillian, was of African, Italian, and Native American descent. She played classical piano at home and gospel music in her church. By marrying our mother, Josefina, he took in the Latin rhythms of her culture. He used all of these influences to create "The Gerald Wilson Sound."

His music is pure jazz yet contains blues, classical, and Latin elements. With the down-home flavor of "Blues for the Count" to the delicacy of his jazz waltz "Blues for Yna Yna," on through to the driving force behind "Viva Tirado," our father felt it all had a place in jazz. From his roots of small town Shelby, Mississippi, our father opened his life to all that the world had to offer and, in turn, expressed that in his music.

(Jeri Wilson, October 2016)

EPILOGUE

Always tell the truth.
—GERALD WILSON

In the summer of 2013, I attended the eighteenth annual Central Avenue Jazz Festival in Los Angeles. The Gerald Wilson Orchestra was the main feature and closing act of the day, and I can say that describing the music, the people, the dancing, and the magical vibes of the orchestra's performance is an eternal description of Gerald and his life.

The orchestra's set at the festival in 2013 was initiated with Gerald's classic "Blues for the Count," at once putting the crowded audience into a nostalgic yet present awareness of swing, blues, suave, and the legacy of Count Basie. Gerald followed with another blues piece, one of his own composed during his Pacific Jazz years, an innovative waltz titled for his children's cat, "Blues for Yna Yna." Another of his classics, the bebop-ish "Triple Chase," was then offered at a very up-tempo pace, featuring among the three saxophone soloists Kamasi Washington, who would eventually land on the cover of Downbeat *in 2016 as the winner of the magazine's international poll for Jazz Album of the Year (*The Epic*). Gerald's "Theme for Monterey" was then performed, with Scott Mayo playing the silky lead melody on soprano sax. Finally, the set closed with what has become Gerald's standard bearer, "Viva Tirado." The crowd yelled, sang out, and danced the late afternoon away. The orchestra had to play it again.*

Gerald Wilson and his orchestra performed the Central Avenue Jazz festival again in 2014; within a few weeks, Gerald passed away. It was, as far as I know, his last or certainly one of his last performances—his final worldly macramé of culture—in his continuing, mystical pilgrimage.

A few days after his passing, when I attended Gerald's rosary and funeral at Holy Cross Cemetery, I was met with love by his wife, Josefina, and his gracious daughters, Jeri and Nancy Jo, his son, Anthony, his grandson Eric, and the rest of his beautiful family. In the Mexican tradition, I wanted to do something special for them, so I cooked a large batch of tamales, and gave them to them at the rosary. I remember seeing Gerald in his casket, with a baseball cap emblazoned with NEA (National Endowment for the Arts) of which he was very proud, as he received the NEA Jazz Master title in 1990; he was at rest, and I felt warmth all around me with his family and friends attending the service.

The next day, meaningful words and tributes were offered in memory of Gerald's life, and as we arrived at the burial place, members of the United States Navy were present to make a tribute to Gerald, including a bugle player who played "Taps" with the soul and energy of Gerald's own spirit. After a few moments, I saw Josefina kiss Gerald's casket and throw a rose into the ground where Gerald was laid to rest. A little less than a year later, she joined him in the same ground. It all made beautiful sense.

Gerald made sense in a world too often beyond sense. He will inspire me and so many others to always go beyond, to always believe, to always love, and—as he always told me and others—to "always tell the truth."

GERALD WILSON SELECTED DISCOGRAPHY

AS LEADER		
Title	**Label; Catalogue No.**	**Publication Date**
Gerald Wilson & His Orchestra: Cruisin' With Gerald	Sounds of Swing Records; LP-121	Unknown
Groovin High in LA—1946 (Benny Carter, Wilbert Baranco, Gerald Wilson, Jimmy Mundy)	Excelsior; 78 159; Reissued 1977, HEP Records; Hep 150	Unknown
Big Band Modern	Audio Lab; AL-1538	1959
Les McCann Sings, Orchestra Under the Direction of Gerald Wilson	Pacific Jazz Records; S T31	1961
You Better Believe It!	Pacific Jazz Records; PJ-34	1961
Gerald Wilson Big Band: Moment of Truth	Pacific Jazz Records; PJ-61	1962
Gerald Wilson Orchestra: Portraits	Pacific Jazz Records; PJ-80	1964
Gerald Wilson Orchestra: On Stage	Pacific Jazz Records; PJ-88	1965
McCann/Wilson: Les McCann & The Gerald Wilson Orchestra	Pacific Jazz; PJ-91	1964
The Wailers: Les McCann & The Gerald Wilson Orchestra	Fontana; 688 150 ZL	1965
Gerald Wilson Orchestra: Feelin' Kinda Blues	Pacific Jazz; PJ-20099	1966
Gerald Wilson Orchestra: The Golden Sword: Torero Impressions in Jazz	Pacific Jazz; PJ-20111	1966

Live and Swinging: The Gerald Wilson Orchestra Plays Standards and Blues	Pacific Jazz; PJ-20118	1967
Gerald Wilson Orchestra: Everywhere	Pacific Jazz; PJ-20132	1968
Gerald Wilson Orchestra: California Soul	Pacific Jazz/World Pacific Jazz; ST-20135	1968
Gerald Wilson Orchestra: Eternal Equinox	Pacific Jazz/World Pacific Jazz; PJ-20160	1969
The Best of Gerald Wilson and His Orchestra	Pacific Jazz; PJ-20174; Reissues: Liberty; SLYL-933856; Pacific Jazz Records; PJ-LA889-H, 1978; United Artists; UA-LA-889, 1978; Mosaic Records; MD5-198, 2000 (5-CD box set)	1970
Gerald Wilson Orchestra of the 80s: Lomelin	Discovery Records; DS-833	1981
Gerald Wilson Orchestra of the 80s: Love You Madly (compilation of *Lomelin* and *Jessica*)	Discovery; DS-947	1981
Gerald Wilson Orchestra of the 80s: Jessica	Trend Records; TR-531	1982
Gerald Wilson Orchestra of the 80s: Calafia	Trend Records; TR-537	1984
Gerald Wilson Orchestra of the 90s: Jenna	Discovery; DS-964	1989
Gerald Wilson Orchestra: State Street Sweet	MAMA Foundation/ Summit Records; 1010	1994
Gerald Wilson and His Orchestra, 1945– 1946	Chronological Classics; 976	1997
Gerald Wilson Orchestra: Theme for Monterey	MAMA/Summit; 1021	1998
The Complete Pacific Jazz Recordings Of Gerald Wilson And His Orchestra	Mosaic Records; MD5-198	2000
Gerald Wilson Orchestra: New York, New Sound	Mack Avenue Records; MAC-1009	2003
Gerald Wilson . . . The Artist Selects	Blue Note/EMI; 31439	2005
Gerald Wilson Orchestra: In My Time	Mack Avenue; MAC-1025	2005
75th Birthday Bash Live!—Kenny Burrell	Blue Note/EMI; 74906	2006
Gerald Wilson and His Orchestra, 1946– 1954	Chronological Classics; 1444	2007

Gerald Wilson Orchestra: Monterey Moods	Mack Avenue; MAC-1039	2007
Solid Sender at the Hepcat's Masquerade: Swing Hot and Cool by Gerald Wilson and His Orchestra	Tuff City	2007
Gerald Wilson Orchestra: Detroit	Mack Avenue; MAC-1049	2009
Gerald Wilson Orchestra: Legacy	Mack Avenue; MAC-1056	2011
You Better Believe It!/Moment Of Truth	American Jazz Classics; AJC-99070	2013
Gerald Wilson and His Orchestra On Jubilee, 1946–1947	Sounds of Yesteryear; 966	2014

AS ARRANGER AND/OR CONDUCTOR FOR OTHER ARTISTS

Artist	Title	Label/No.	Date	Wilson's Role
Ray Charles	Modern Sounds in Country and Western Music	ABC-Paramount; ABC 410	1962	Arranger
Ray Charles	Modern Sounds in Country and Western Music—Volume 2	ABC-Paramount; ABC 435	1962	Arranger
Bobby Darin	You're the Reason I'm Living	Capitol Records; ST 1866	1963	Arranger
Sarah Vaughan	Sarah Sings Soulfully	Roulette; SR 52116	1963	Arranger
Nancy Wilson	Yesterday's Love Songs/ Today's Blues	Capitol Records; ST 2012	1963	Arranger and Conductor
Ray Charles	Have a Smile with Me	ABC-Paramount; ABC 495	1964	Arranger
Nancy Wilson	Broadway—My Way	Capitol Records; T 1828	1964	Arranger and Conductor
Al Hirt	Live at Carnegie Hall	RCA Victor; LSP-3416	1965	Arranger
Julie London	Feeling Good	Liberty; LBY 1281	1965	Arranger and Conductor

David Axelrod	*Songs of Experience*	Capitol Records; SKAO-338	1969	Arranger
Jean-Luc Ponty	*Electric Connection*	World Pacific Jazz; ST-20156	1969	Arranger and Conductor
Ella Fitzgerald	*Things Ain't What They Used to Be (And You Better Believe It)*	Reprise; RS 6432	1970	Arranger and Conductor
Kenny Burrell	*75th Birthday Bash Live!*	Blue Note/EMI; 74906	2006	Arranger and Conductor

AS SIDEMAN ON TRUMPET

Artist	Title	Label/No.	Release Date
Duke Ellington	*Dance to the Duke!*	Capitol Records; T-637	1954
Buddy Collette	*Buddy Collette: Man of Many Parts*	Contemporary; C3522	1956
Curtis Counce	*Carl's Blues*	Contemporary; M3574/ S7574	1960
Leroy Vinnegar	*Leroy Walks!* By the Leroy Vinnegar Sextet	Contemporary; C3542	1958
Duke Ellington	*Anatomy of a Murder* Film soundtrack	Columbia; CL 1360	1959
Duke Ellington	*Swinging Suites by Edward E. and Edward G.*	Columbia; CS 8397	1960
Curtis Counce	*Sonority*	Contemporary; C7655	1989

SPOKEN WORD

Title	Label/No.	Release Date
Suite Memories: Reflections on a Jazz Journey: A Spoken-Word Double Album & Scrapbook	MAMA Foundation/ Summit; 1014	1996

REFERENCES

Agawu, Kofi. 2003. *Representing African Music: Postcolonial Notes, Queries, Positions.* New York and London: Routledge.

Saint Augustine. 1958. *City of God.* Trans. Gerald G. Walsh, SJ, Demetrius B. Zema, SJ, Grace Monahan, OSU, and Daniel J. Honan. New York: Image Books, Doubleday & Company.

Briggs, Ray. 2005. Liner notes. *Gerald Wilson Orchestra: In My Time.* Grosse Pointe Farms, MI: Mack Avenue. MAC1025.

Clarke, Donald. 2002. *Billie Holiday: Wishing On the Moon.* Cambridge, MA: Da Capo Press.

Cook, Stephen. 1962. Liner notes. *Modern Sounds in Country and Western Music.* New York: ABC Paramount Records. ABC 410.

Croce, Benedetto. 1965. *Guide to aesthetics (Breviario di estetica).* Trans. Patrick Romanell. Indianapolis: Bobbs-Merrill.

Davis, Angela Y. 1999. *Blues Legacies and Black Feminism: Gertrude "Ma" Rainey, Bessie Smith and Billie Holiday.* New York: Vintage.

Du Bois, W. E. B. 1990. *The Souls of Black Folk.* New York: Vintage Books/Library of America.

Feather, Leonard. 1981. Liner notes. *Lomelin.* Los Angeles: Discovery Records. DS833.

Feld, Steven. 2012. *Jazz Cosmopolitanism in Accra: Five Musical Years in Ghana.* Durham and London: Duke University Press.

Floyd, Samuel A., Jr. 1995. *The Power of Black Music.* New York and Oxford: Oxford University Press.

Freire, Paulo. 1985 (1968). *Pedagogy of the Oppressed.* Trans. Myra Bergman Ramos. New York: Continuum.

Gardner, Barbara. 1963. Liner notes. Nancy Wilson: Yesterday's Love Songs . . . Today's Blues. Capitol Records. ST 2012.

Ginell, Richard S. Biography. http://www.allmusic.com/artist/gerald-wilson-mn0000 946171.

Gioia, Ted. 1992. *West Coast Jazz: Modern Jazz in California, 1945–1960.* New York and Oxford: Oxford University Press.

Gramsci, Antonio, Quintin Hoare, and Geoffrey Nowell-Smith. 1971. *Selections from the Prison Notebooks of Antonio Gramsci*. New York: International Publishers.

Gridley, Mark. C., with contributions by David Cutler. 2003. *Jazz Styles: History and Analysis*. Upper Saddle River, NJ: Prentice Hall.

Gruzinski, Serge. 2002. *The Mestizo Mind: The Intellectual Dynamics of Colonization and Globalization*. Trans. Deke Dusinberre. London and New York: Routledge.

Guillén, Nicolás. 1980. *Motivos de son*. Havana: Editorial Letras Cubanas.

Heckman, Don. 2014. "Gerald Wilson Dies at 96; Multifaceted Jazz Musician." *Los Angeles Times*, September 8.

hooks, bell, and Cornel West. 1999. "The Dilemma of the Black Intellectual." In *The Cornel West Reader*, 302–315. New York: Basic Books. Originally published in *Culture Critique* 1, no. 1 (1985) and republished in *Breaking Bread: Insurgent Black Intellectual Life*, by bell hooks and Cornel West (Cambridge, MA: South End Press, 1991, pp. 131–46).

Jackson, Travis A. 2012. *Blowin' the Blues Away: Performance and Meaning on the New York Jazz Scene*. Berkeley, Los Angeles, and London: University of California Press.

Jones, LeRoi (Amiri Baraka). 1970. *Black Music*. New York: William Morrow & Company.

———. 1963. *Blues People: The Negro Experience in White America and the Music that Developed From It*. New York: William Morrow & Company.

Kelley, Robin D. G. 1999. "The People in Me." *Utne Reader* 95 (September): 79–81.

Levin, Robert. 1963. Liner notes. *Outward Bound* by Eric Dolphy. Prestige. 7311.

Lomax, Alan. 1950. *Mister Jelly Roll: The Fortunes of Jelly Roll Morton, New Orleans Creole and "Inventor of Jazz."* New York: Grosset and Dunlap.

Lowe, Lisa. 1996. *Immigrant Acts: On Asian American Cultural Politics*. Durham, NC: Duke University Press.

Marx, Albert. 1983. Liner notes. *Jessica*. Los Angeles: Discovery Trend Records. TR531.

McFarland, Pancho. 2008. *Chicano Rap: Gender and Violence in the Postindustrial Barrio*. Austin: University of Texas Press.

Minh-ha, Trinh T. *Naked Spaces: Living Is Round* film directed by Minh-ha – info?

Molina, Ruben. 2007. *Chicano Soul: Recordings and History of an American Culture*. Los Angeles: Mictlan Publishing.

Mosaic Records. 2003 (January). Brochure, 47, 33.

Murray, Albert. 1970. *The Omni-Americans: New Perspectives on Black Experience and American Culture*. New York: Outerbridge and Dienstfrey.

New York Times. "Teddy Wilson Dies; Pianist and Leader of 30's Jazz Combos," August 1, 1986.

Pérez-Torres, Rafael. 2006. *Mestizaje: Critical Uses of Race in Chicano Culture*. Minneapolis: University of Minnesota Press.

Ramsey, Doug. 2000. Liner booklet. *The Complete Pacific Jazz Recordings of Gerald Wilson and His Orchestra*. Mosaic Records (EMI-Capitol Music Special Markets). MD5–198.

Reig, Teddy. 1963. Liner notes, *Sarah Sings Soulfully: Sarah Vaughan.* Roulette Birdland Records. R-52116.

Reyes, David, and Tom Waldman. 2009. *Land of a Thousand Dances: Chicano Rock 'n' Roll from Southern California.* Albuquerque: University of New Mexico Press.

Robles Cahero, José Antonio. 2003. "Occidentalización, mestizaje y "guerra de los sonidos": hacia una historia de las musicas mestizas de México." In *Musical Cultures of Latin America: Global Effects, Past and Present,* ed. Steven Joseph Loza, 39–56. UCLA Ethnomusicology Publications, University of California, Los Angeles.

Rodríguez, Luís J. 2001, 2014. *Hearts and Hands: Connecting Community in Violent Times.* New York: Seven Stories Press.

Saranich, Ron. 2005. Review of *In My Time,* by Gerald Wilson and His Orchestra. Cosmik Reviews. http://www.cosmik.com/aa-april-july07/reviews/review_gerald _wilson.html.

Sheridan, Chris. 1992, 2006. Liner notes. *Groovin' High in L.A.: Benny Carter, Wilbert Baranco, Gerald Wilson, Jimmy Mundy and Their Orchestras.* United Kingdom: Hep Records.

Shipton, Alyn. 2001. *A New History of Jazz.* London and New York: Continuum.

Silsbee, Kirk. 1998. Liner notes. *Gerald Wilson Orchestra: Theme for Monterey.* Simi Valley, California: MAMA Records (MAMA Foundation). MMF 1021.

———. 1996. Liner notes. *Gerald Wilson: Suite Memories: Reflections On a Jazz Journey* (spoken-word album). Simi Valley, California: MAMA Foundation.

Simosko, Vladimir, and Barry Tepperman. 1979. *Eric Dolphy: A Musical Biography and Discography.* New York: Da Capo Press.

Small, Christopher. 1987. *Music of the Common Tongue: Survival and Celebration in African American Music.* London: Calder; New York: Riverrun Press.

Starr, Larry, and Christopher Alan Waterman. 2010. *American Popular Music: From Minstrelsy to MP3.* New York and Oxford: Oxford University Press.

Stewart, Zan. 2009. Liner notes. *Gerald Wilson Orchestra: Detroit.* Grosse Pointe Farms, MI: Mack Avenue Records. MAC 1049

———. 2002. "Orchestral Man: Gerald Wilson Excites with His Complex Sounds." *Downbeat,* March, 40–43.

Tapscott, Horace. 2001. *Songs of the Unsung: The Musical and Social Journey of Horace Tapscott,* ed. Steven Isoardi. Durham and London: Duke University Press.

Tesser, Neil. 2011. Liner notes. *Legacy: Gerald Wilson Orchestra.* Grosse Pointe Farms, MI: Mack Avenue Records, MAC1056.

Turner, Victor. 1977. *The Ritual Process: Structure and Anti-Structure.* Ithaca and New York: Cornell University Press.

Vercelli, Gary G. 1995. Liner notes. *Gerald Wilson Orchestra: State Street Sweet.* Simi Valley, CA: Mama Foundation. MMF 1010.

Walser, Robert. 1999. *Keeping Time: Readings in Jazz History.* New York and Oxford: Oxford University Press.

Walton, Ortiz. 1972. *Music: Black, White, and Blue.* New York: William Morrow & Company.

West, Cornel. 1999. "On Afro-American Music: From Bebop to Rap." In *The Cornel West Reader*, 474–85. New York, NY: Basic Books.

Williams, Martin. 1970. *The Jazz Tradition*. New York: Oxford University Press.

Wilson, Gerald. 1996. *Gerald Wilson: Suite Memories: Reflections on a Jazz Journey* (spoken-word album). Simi Valley, California: MAMA Foundation.

——. 1991. Interview by Stephen Isoardi. In "Central Avenue Sounds." Oral History Program, Department of Special Collections, University of California, Los Angeles.

——. 2001. Interviews conducted by Steven Loza.

Yang, Mina. 2008. *California Polyphony: Ethnic Voices, Musical Crossroads*. Urbana and Chicago: University of Illinois Press.

Yanow, Scott. 2007. Liner notes. *Gerald Wilson Orchestra: Monterey Moods*. Mack Avenue Records. MAC1039.

Yardley, William. 2014. "Gerald Wilson, Versatile Jazz Arranger, Is Dead at 96." *New York Times*, September 9.

INDEX

179

CPSIA information can be obtained
at www.ICGtesting.com
Printed in the USA
BVHW03s0732130318
510013BV00001B/2/P

9 781496 817389